More Praise fo

"I am honored to review this fi𝑒 ..., _____ ...ɔ𝖼ɪntɪngly courageous memoir. As a psycho-oncologist for over forty years, I
found Reba's account of Hannah's final illness to be honest and
insightful enough to be of use for other families going through
joining, as she puts it, 'the club no parent wants to belong to.'"

—John Edward Ruark, MD, EFACP, retired adjunct clinical
    associate professor of psychiatry, Stanford University
    School of Medicine

"Looking at the loss of her young daughter from an astrological
and soul perspective, Reba Ferguson bravely recounts the story
of a special mother-daughter relationship interrupted by illness
but not broken by death. Reba's healing journey includes visits
with astrologers and mediums who deepen her understanding
while affirming the unbroken connection with her daughter."

—Linda "Moonrabbit" Zlotnick, author of _Star Sisters:
    An Astrological Memoir of Twin Loss_

"A powerful, heartbreaking window into a mother's grief and
despair and her determination to find hope and healing in the
aftermath of her only daughter's death. Reba offers the reader
an inside look at the world of pediatric cancer and its devastat-
ing impact on a child, a family, and a community."

—Margo Fowkes, Founder, Salt Water (findyourharbor.com)

"Honesty. Healing. Hope. In that order. One step leads to the
next one if we can be brave enough to tell the truth. In _A Soul
Lives On_ Reba Ferguson tells her story with vulnerable authen-
ticity and humility. Sometimes telling the truth about the
wounds and grief in our lives is impossible. Sometimes it is the
only thing we can possibly do."

—The Reverend William Harper, Vicar Emeritus,
    Grace Church, Bainbridge Island, Washington

"With remarkable courage, Reba Ferguson shows us that the most gut-wrenching of losses can be met with honesty and self-compassion. *A Soul Lives On* invites us into a mother-daughter love story of gratitude, grief, understanding, and hope—an affirmation of how one child's life and death transformed the lives of so many others."

—Marilyn Price-Mitchell, PhD, developmental psychologist

"Ever since my husband passed almost five years ago, I have had a hard time focusing my mind to read a book. Not true with *A Soul Lives On*. I read it in two days—I couldn't put it down. Reba has a keen ability to transfer feelings of grief to pages. I found this book raw, honest, love-packed. We witness two souls joining as one through pain, loss, and love. Great love does great things. Read it and be moved."

—The Reverend Rosella Sims

A Soul Lives On

A MOTHER'S MEMOIR OF GRIEF, ASTROLOGY, AND THE AFTERLIFE

Reba Ferguson

Libra Moon Press

A Soul Lives On: A Mother's Memoir of Grief, Astrology, and the Afterlife
Published by Libra Moon Press, Bainbridge Island, WA

Print ISBN 978-0-578-99302-7
E-book ISBN 978-0-578-99303-4
Library of Congress Control Number: 2021920149

A percentage of the proceeds of this book will be donated in Hannah's memory to Seattle Children's Pediatric Brain Tumor Research Fund.

To learn more about the author, visit:
rebaferguson.com

Cover design by Christian Storm
Cover art by Bill Hunt
Author photo by Deanna Dusabek
Page design by Beth Wright, Wright for Writers LLC

The lyrics in chapter 33 are from the song "Safe" by Erin Austin copyright © Riptide Music Group, LLC. All rights reserved. Used by permission.

for Hannah

Contents

Preface

Where there is great love, there are always miracles.
—Willa Cather

When my twelve-year-old daughter died of a brain tumor, my heart was shattered. It was inconceivable to me that she was gone, and I didn't know if I would be able to survive the loss. But then hope came from the most unexpected places. Comfort from other women who understood my grief. Solace in the stars. Proof of an afterlife. In her death, my daughter gave me my life back.

1

A Seed Is Planted

I was born six weeks early, on my mom's birthday, with a hole in my heart. For some reason, I came rushing into this world needing to be healed. The physical defect resolved on its own. I never worried about the status of my heart when I was young. But when I became an adult, and later a mom myself, I began to wonder if it was a precursor of something deeper in my soul. Had I been an ancient stargazer, I might have seen it as an omen.

Fast-forward to my thirty-seventh year. I was now a wife and a mother of two living on an island in the Pacific Northwest. My dad had died ten years earlier of a sudden heart attack, leaving my mom alone in the Midwest house where my brother and I had grown up. My husband was a busy and successful Realtor, making it challenging for us to take vacations, especially in the summer. But in June 1996, we found a way to get off the island for a long weekend without our young boys.

The phone rang just as Bill and I walked into the house, having returned from our weekend getaway. "Hi Reba. It's Pat." My mom's best friend was calling, and she didn't sound good. Without her normal friendly tone, she hesitated before saying, "Your mom's not doing well. You'd better get back here."

Mom was in a hospital in Cincinnati, recovering from elective knee replacement surgery. At age sixty-nine, she had decided to have this procedure to improve her mobility. My brother, Claude, and I lived on opposite ends of the country, while our widowed mom still lived in our hometown. She had invited my brother to be with her for the surgery.

I was farther away, with two little boys, so that made some sense. Although Mom and I didn't have a particularly close relationship, I felt the sting of my younger brother being the favored one.

After Claude left Mom in the hospital to return to his work and family, she didn't recover as the doctors expected. When Pat called to tell me to come home, a voice inside me said, *Go*, so I flew out to be with her. The day after I arrived, Mom suffered a postoperative bleed and had to go into intensive care. Never again would I think of a simple procedure as simple.

Over the next nine months, Claude and his wife, Linda, took turns with me sitting with Mom in the ICU; my aunts, uncles, female cousins, and Pat also visited. Since my brother and I had to travel back and forth to see her, I was relieved that we had backup. Still, I hated leaving my boys, so young at two and four years old. My husband frantically tried to keep his business going while caring for the boys when I was gone. Some friends helped out, but it was tough. Every time I got on a late ferry from my island home in the Puget Sound to catch the red-eye flight to Ohio, I cried at having to leave my family. It was an exhausting ordeal.

On one of my frequent visits to Mom, I told her, "I'm thinking of having another baby." Unable to speak, since she was hooked up to a ventilator, she looked at me with wide eyes. Mom knew how difficult pregnancy had been for me, including all-day morning sickness for nine months. What she didn't realize at first was that this idea to have a baby, hopefully a baby girl, had been seeded right there in the hospital, because of her.

"If I hadn't seen the women in our family surrounding you here in the hospital, it maybe wouldn't have occurred to me. Now I want to try to have a daughter," I explained.

I'd seen firsthand how the women in Mom's life had lovingly cared for her. Those intense months of going back and forth to the hospital had also led me to stronger connections with the women in my life, something I had missed with my mom. For the first time, I realized that it was the women in our lives who give birth and who help people die.

Four months after I had this conversation with Mom, she died. Despite my grief, my relief that her suffering was over, and my hesitancy about having another baby, I continued to dream of having a girl of my own. I couldn't escape this idea of having a daughter with whom I could share my heart, not to mention someone who might take care of me at the end of my life. The idea of having another baby waxed and waned. Bill was supportive of my dream but left the final decision to me. We already had three boys, including our older son, Adam, from Bill's first marriage. Although Adam was nearly grown at seventeen and lived with his mom in California, another child, possibly another boy, felt like a lot.

Still, I kept hearing a small voice inside my head—a soul, I believed—telling me that she wanted to come into our family. I talked with my girlfriends about it. I especially remember talking with a family friend and minister who seemed to read my heart and invited me to talk about this soul who I sensed wanted to be part of our lives. But the reality of life kept getting in the way, and I kept dismissing the idea, particularly given how difficult my pregnancies had been. Even so, if we were going to have another baby, I really wanted a girl. We hadn't cared what gender our first two babies were; in fact, we hadn't even planned their births. But with the possibility of a new life, I wanted to do everything I could to ensure that we would have a girl.

I did some of the things a friend who had also wanted a girl had done to try to skew the odds. I tracked my cycle and took my temperature daily to know when I was ovulating. I adjusted my diet to a healthy "girl-inducing" regimen for a while. Doing these things gave me the illusion that I had control over choosing my child's sex, but in the end, I believe that I was fated to have a daughter and that I merely said yes to a soul who wanted to be with us.

After months of waffling and temperature taking, Bill and I were still undecided. On Halloween we held a party at our house for friends and their children. In the midst of the festivities we learned that another friend had just delivered a baby boy. I turned to Bill, and together we said, "Let's go for it!" I knew my body well by then; it was an optimal time in my cycle to try for a girl.

Turns out, I was pregnant the next day, November 1—a significant day in the Christian calendar, known as All Saints' Day, when the veil between this world and the next is very thin. My daughter was conceived eight months after Mom passed away—about the same gestational time she carried me. After the extremely difficult year we'd had with my mom's illness and death, I was overjoyed to be expecting a baby, hopefully a baby girl. A new seed, a new life, a new soul had been planted.

In the meantime, Claude and Linda had decided to move to the Pacific Northwest, in large part because they wanted to be close to our family after Mom died. I was thrilled that they would be living on our island, that we would be part of each other's lives, and that the cousins would grow up together. Their three children would soon join Ryan and Andrew, plus the baby I was expecting. I couldn't have been happier.

When Hannah was born in the summer of 1998, she was a healthy, nearly ten-pound baby girl, seemingly perfect in every way.

Our wedding with Mom, Claude, Linda,
and young Chris, 1990

Bill and I with Ryan and Andrew during Mom's illness, 1996

2

A Death in the Family

It was a hot July day in the summer of 2007 when we got the call we'd been anticipating. Bill's mom, Ann, had died. Fairly quickly, we loaded our three kids into the car and drove from our island home near Seattle to Weaverville, a small, blue-collar town in Northern California where Bill grew up with his mom, dad, and three older brothers. We seldom saw Bill's family, meeting maybe once every few years, but they were fun and easy to be with. On the trip down Hannah, who was now nine years old, asked a lot of questions about her grandma and the family she barely knew. While I wasn't looking forward to saying goodbye to Ann, I was happy that the occasion was cause for a family reunion.

Arriving at Ann's home days after her death, we faced the task of sorting through her belongings and packing up her small house. Having helped with my grandparents' house when I was nine and my parents' house thirty years later, after Mom died, I was all too familiar with the job of sorting and dispensing a loved one's earthly possessions. Ryan and Andrew, now teenagers, seemed bored and were not so helpful with the whole boxing-and-cleaning affair. But Hannah dove right in to help. She hadn't known Grandma Ann very well, but she quickly gravitated to the things of hers she loved—stuffed animals, old nail polish, and costume jewelry.

Hannah had always loved dressing up and pretending to be older than she was. For years I had collected secondhand dresses and jewelry for her to play with during time with her friends. She would spend hours in her room, alone or with a girlfriend, trying on clothes and different hairstyles while dancing and singing to pop music. Eventually she would come downstairs to strut around the kitchen in too-big shoes, pretending to be a model or a dancer and smiling from ear to ear. These dress-up skills prepared her for her dance recitals, starting at age three. Initially she needed my help to plaster her long blond hair atop her head, but before long she was doing her own dance hair and makeup quite well, in a flattering and age-appropriate manner. Hannah could go from goofy to grownup in a heartbeat.

At Grandma Ann's, Hannah sat in the bedroom in front of a lighted makeup mirror, just as she had done backstage. She was content to play by herself, trying on pieces of jewelry, only coming out to show me something when she was really excited about it. One afternoon, she came running into the kitchen where I was sorting through dishes to tell me, "Look what I found!" Hannah was wearing Ann's good amethyst ring, which was too big on her index finger. "Can I keep it?" she asked.

"Wow, that's really pretty. We'd better ask your cousins if anyone else is interested in it," I said.

The family decided on a raffle system to divide up beloved and valuable pieces. When I was lucky enough to win the drawing for Ann's ring, I figured the heirloom piece would someday belong to Hannah.

We enjoyed spending that time with Bill's brothers and their families. Our kids loved the chance to see their oldest brother, Adam, as well as their much-admired older cousins. We stayed at Uncle Steve and Aunt Jeanne's house. Hannah adored being a mother's helper to their two-year-old grandson. In the hundred-degree sunshine, she spent hours blowing bubbles and entertaining him in a small plastic pool. When she was even younger, Hannah had loved playing with her baby dolls. She told me over and over again that she couldn't wait to be a mother.

When Bill and the boys started a backyard whiffle ball game, Hannah jumped right in, just as she had done countless times at home. She loved nothing more than showing off her strength and fierceness as she took her stance at the plate. "Let's see what you've got!" she yelled to Andrew, the pitcher. She had grown up in the shadow of her athletic brothers, who inspired her to excel at physical sports, such as dance and soccer.

Hannah was more of a peacemaker than a competitor among her girlfriends. The summer before, on her eighth birthday, she had invited her six closest friends to celebrate with her at our house. Most of the girls thought of Hannah as their best friend. For her party, I didn't need to provide anything but the food and the birthday cake. Hannah did the rest as the girls went from one activity to another—singing and dancing in her bedroom, jumping on the backyard trampoline, scootering in the driveway, splashing in the hot tub on our back deck, watching a movie in the evening while crammed together on the den couch, and giggling late into the night as they resisted falling asleep.

A couple of the girls, jealous and eager to be number one with Hannah, fought for her attention that day. She did her best to dispel the tension with humor and a distracting activity. "C'mon guys, let's go downstairs and have ice cream and cake!" She wanted everyone to get along.

When I was pregnant with Hannah, I'd had few expectations about the kind of person she would become. As it turned out, she was a more loving, engaging, and inspiring daughter than I ever dreamed she would be. I felt so lucky to be raising this spunky, independent girl, whom I totally adored. From an early age she invited friends to be with her, not waiting for an invitation or for me to set up playdates. By age four she had memorized girls' phone numbers so she could call them herself. At school she had a variety of friends, adapting her personality to whomever she was with. She mostly stayed out of exclusive groups or cliques, keeping company with the popular girls but also spending time with those who had trouble socializing. In the classroom or on the playground, she was often the leader of the pack simply because girls wanted to be near her.

As she got older, she was open and talkative with her girlfriends. She didn't shy away from sharing her heart or encouraging others to do the same. She helped her friends when they were down. When she became aware of difficult dynamics and dramas among her friends, she would try to work it out on her own, but when she couldn't solve it, she brought it to me. I learned a lot from my daughter.

Hannah brought the same friendly ease to Weaverville as we said goodbye to Bill's mother. Each evening, we all gathered around the backyard picnic table under the lights of the porch. Hannah never missed the nightly poker game, a Hunt family tradition. As with most things she did, she learned poker early and was very good at it. She more than held her own, making bets and taking cards among the guys around the table, with an instinct that couldn't be taught. I didn't usually join in, but I loved watching the play, along with the card-table banter and laughter. I would hear Hannah say, "Read 'em and weep," as she dealt out cards for Texas hold 'em.

"I see you and I raise you," she ribbed Bill, who just laughed back at her challenge.

"Now let's see what you've got!" he said.

"Full house!" she yelled in victory as she flung her arms around her dad and kissed him on the cheek. Hannah loved the connection with her brothers and the adults around the table.

Ann's funeral was held at her Catholic church, a small white building on a hill in town, on a gorgeous, blue-sky day. The younger boys wore casual shirts; twenty-seven-year-old Adam wore a suit and tie. Hannah initially pouted because I had brought a white, frilly, old-fashioned dress for her. She saw herself as an older, fashionable preteen. "I'm not a little girl!" she said, scowling.

For the most part we got along well, but this wasn't the first time we'd butted heads. Hannah seldom hesitated to tell me what she thought or how she felt. I was familiar with her eye rolls and snarky remarks when she was unhappy with me. As usual, it didn't last long. By the time we entered the church for the service, her grumpy mood had faded and she sat next to me in the pew. This was the first funeral she'd attended, and in this unfamiliar space she seemed to need the comfort of my close presence. When Uncle Dave stood and tearfully spoke about his mom, Hannah grabbed my hand and squeezed it hard.

I loved Ann, but it was hard to see how miserable and feeble she'd become in the last years of her life. I hadn't known the formerly healthy woman whom my daughter took after: high-spirited, strong, and independent. Ann was diagnosed with throat cancer in 1990, right before Bill and I were married. Part of her treatment included a laryngectomy. For a social and talkative woman, this was a huge loss. Bill recalled his mom saying, before she got sick, "The absolute worst thing I could imagine would be losing my voice." He replied, at the time, "The worst thing I could imagine would be losing a child."

In the years preceding her death, Ann's life had become progressively difficult, but it wasn't without love. As she grew sicker and more disabled, her boys supported her in her own small house in the hometown where she had raised them. Seeing Ann grow increasingly dependent made me sad for my own mom. Her catastrophic illness seemed far more tragic because she was much younger than Ann when she died. Mom was never able to return to her own home, let alone be cared for by her children in her final years. And she never got to meet my daughter. At least I could be thankful to Mom for giving me the gift of Hannah.

Ann's memorial marked the first time all ten Hunt cousins had come together in one place since Hannah, the youngest, had been born. During the reception, I lined up the brothers and their kids for pictures. Hannah stood in the center, holding the newborn baby of her oldest cousin, Heather. No longer bothered by her dress, Hannah was full of smiles for the camera and so happy to be with her family, to see Adam, and to play with her cousins. No one knew that it was the last time the group would be together.

Jade and Hannah playing dress-up,
2001

A Hunt family poker game with Grandma Ann, 2004

Hunt brothers and cousins at Ann's service, 2007

Our family in Steve and Jeanne's backyard

3

Something Is Seriously Wrong

L ater that year, Halloween—Hannah's second-favorite holiday, after Christmas—was approaching. She was in the fourth grade. Every day after school meant dance classes, soccer practice, and homework. The weekends were for soccer games, playdates, and sleepovers. Hannah was especially excited about the upcoming Wilkes carnival, an annual Halloween event for the school in which the fourth graders played a special part. She attended meetings with friends to prepare for the haunted house and couldn't wait for the fun day.

After gathering costumes and props, Hannah spent the night at a girlfriend's while Bill and I were out to dinner. The friend's mom called me to say, "Hannah's not feeling well. I gave her some cough syrup, and she went back to sleep. She didn't want to go home. Just wanted to let you know." I wasn't surprised to hear that Hannah wanted to stay; she never wanted to leave a friend's house unless she had to.

The next day, Hannah had a soccer game. Bill and I met her at the field where her friends dropped her off. She seemed fine. We stood on the sidelines with coffee in hand, watching the game as usual. Hannah was playing defense, her normal position. During a goal kick, she ran up to kick the ball and flat-out missed it rather than booting it down the field as usual. "Hmm, that was strange. Maybe she's in the midst of a growth spurt," I said to Bill.

Toward the end of the game, Hannah was involved in a skirmish in front of the goal. All of a sudden she was lying on the ground. She had twisted her ankle and came limping off the field to me, crying in pain.

That was weird too. Normally she toughed out any small injury and kept playing. She wasn't like some of the girls on the team who cried at the smallest thing. Hannah sat with me for the remainder of the game.

When snacks came out, I asked her if she wanted a juice or a granola bar. She said, "I don't feel good. I feel sick." She stayed slumped in my lap with her head down. After a game, she usually ran off with her girl-friends to the playground. But that day she slowly walked back to the car with me instead.

The following day, Hannah woke up with a horrible headache. It seemed to take a lot of Tylenol to get rid of it. The same thing happened the next day, causing her to miss school. As the week wore on more symptoms presented themselves—dizziness, nausea, and a stagger-ing gait. It was odd to watch her slow, stuttering walk from one point to another, with abrupt stops to catch herself from falling. I had never seen Hannah have poor balance. Then, with another headache, Han-nah lay in my lap in agony. "I feel like I'm dying," she groaned. I rubbed her back and tried to comfort her as I stroked her long, silky blond hair. I was starting to think that something was seriously wrong with my daughter.

Over the next two weeks, Hannah and I made multiple trips to our local clinic to try to get to the bottom of her symptoms. The doctors tossed around several diagnoses over a number of appointments—a virus, an ear infection, or vertigo—but they could never say for sure. During one urgent visit, a doctor we hadn't seen before seemed espe-cially troubled by Hannah's symptoms. His conclusion was that she had some kind of virus, but his suspicions and call to a consulting physician only fueled my worry.

One day Courtney, one of Hannah's best friends, came over to play. Hannah usually had boundless energy, loving nothing more than com-ing up with countless fun activities with her friends. But that day, Han-nah couldn't do much but lie on the couch. Then I noticed a new and troubling symptom: her eyes had started to cross. I had never seen Han-nah's eyes do that before, and it was very disturbing. I went upstairs to my bedroom, closed the door, and lay down on the bed. *Hannah is getting worse,* I thought. I tried to calm my racing heart, but I knew this wasn't good. It was almost too alarming to tell Bill, but I did later that day, when Courtney went home.

We showed up at the clinic first thing in the morning. After some preliminary questions, the doctor immediately ordered a CAT scan of Hannah's head. I didn't think much of it as Hannah and I climbed into the mobile CT van in the clinic's parking lot. I didn't start to freak out until a whole slew of folks walked into the exam room with the results of the scan. The doctor didn't hesitate to say the words: "It's a brain tumor."

My world crumbled. "What?" I burst into tears and then couldn't catch my breath. I began to shiver and felt an ice-cold knife piercing my heart. *My daughter can't die.* I could barely stand the thought. *How can I lose her? How can I grow old without her? How did this happen?* Death was staring me in the face.

For a while I couldn't speak. When the doctor asked if she could call someone, I said, "Yes, call Bill." *I can't do this alone.*

Bill appeared within minutes and held me, held Hannah. She was almost giddy to have her dad join us. Now, hearing a diagnosis of what was wrong, I couldn't stop the tears, feeling with certainty that death was knocking at the door. I couldn't stop the screaming in my brain. I could barely hear the instructions from the clinic staff as they directed us to go immediately to Children's Hospital.

Riding to the ferry, with Bill driving and Hannah in the back seat, I began to collect myself. I needed to call Linda to take care of Ryan and Andrew after school. I needed my friend Jeanette to meet me at Children's. But no one else. The news was too awful to share. *My daughter has a brain tumor.*

During the ferry crossing, I hunkered down in the car while Bill took Hannah upstairs to walk around on the boat. I couldn't see anyone. I had just heard the worst news in my life. I couldn't possibly run into someone I knew. I took a deep breath and made the two phone calls.

Linda didn't seem to hear what I was telling her. She said she wasn't sure she could help with the boys. It didn't seem to register with her at all that Hannah could be seriously ill. Jeanette didn't hesitate: "I'll meet you at the hospital." And then I sat alone, shivering and crying in the car. *I can't do this. I don't want to do this.*

Random odd thoughts entered my mind. *My perfect daughter is no longer perfect. Someone please take this away from me. What good can come of this? Maybe I will lose ten pounds. There's a bright spot.* I was signed up for snacks at school. *Who do I call? I'm wearing sweats and a long-sleeved T-shirt. How long will I be at the hospital? What do I need there? Who will take care of the dogs today?* My manager self tried to write a mental to-do list, but it kept getting washed away by tsunamis of sadness and grief.

We arrived at Seattle Children's. Jeanette joined us as soon as we got there. Years ago, I had been the calm presence for her during her breast cancer surgeries. Now I needed her to be there for me. After we had waited hours, the staff did an extensive MRI of Hannah's brain and spine. The pictures showed a golf ball–sized tumor in the back of her head. Surgery was scheduled for the next day.

At first Hannah was calm. That evening, when we were finally checked into her private room on the surgical floor, she acted as if she was staying in a fancy hotel with room service. One of the young residents who came in to describe the surgery to her reminded us of Grant, the young man who had babysat Hannah and her brothers the previous summer. Grant and Hannah had bonded through playing board games, watching TV shows, and talking. The doctor had a charming bedside manner and helped distract Hannah from thinking about the surgery.

She fell asleep fairly easily that night, while Bill and I collapsed in her room on the couch-turned-bed. We held each other and cried, wondering out loud how our world had suddenly turned so dark and scary. In the middle of the night, Hannah woke up, worried that her friends wouldn't come to see her in the hospital and that she might look different after surgery. Hannah finally released some of her fears, but she didn't know the scope of possibilities I was storing in my head.

When Hannah was carted off for the eight-hour neurosurgery, I fell into my friends' and family's arms. I had mostly held it together after the initial shock in the clinic exam room, but now I could let out all of my fears. We received periodic updates from the surgical team that Hannah was handling surgery as they expected. But the procedure seemed to drag on forever.

Finally it was over. After we talked briefly with the surgeon, we went to see Hannah in the ICU. I don't know what I thought I'd see, maybe a bald-headed girl, but here was Hannah looking like Hannah, just not yet conscious. While she continued to sleep, I nearly passed out in her room, feeling a tingling in the back of my head along with an increasing burden of fear and anxiety. And I had NOT heard the words I had hoped to hear from her neurosurgeon, that the tumor was probably benign.

Sleep-deprived from weeks of staying up late with my very ill daughter, I slept that night on a little bench in her ICU room, mostly unaware of the comings and goings of the nurses and doctors. I missed the moment when Hannah finally woke up from the anesthesia. When I went to her bedside to talk with her, she was delirious, moody, and not really aware of what had happened to her. She looked angry and confused and didn't seem to know where she was. I said, "Hannah, you're in the ICU. You're recovering from brain surgery. You're going to be okay." But no matter what I said, I couldn't seem to find the words to calm her down.

Minutes later, Bill came in the room. He'd spent the night in the hospital's sleeping room for parents. Hannah began yelling at him for no apparent reason. She started screaming, "Get out! Get out! Get out! I don't want to see you!" She didn't seem to recognize him. Bill backed off, turned around toward me, and with tears in his eyes said, "I don't know what to do." Almost on cue, Adam, who had arrived the night before, walked in the room. He seemed to have the magic touch with his sister. He stood by her bed and talked softly to her, and she quieted down. For whatever reason, Hannah responded to Adam's voice.

I stood at the foot of the bed, looking out the window with tears streaming down my face. I couldn't even look at my daughter. I couldn't believe what I was seeing—Hannah in an ICU bed, surrounded by monitors and IV poles, yelling at her dad, upset and frustrated. *Who is this girl? What's happened to Hannah?*

Soccer with friend, Riley, before diagnosis, fall 2007

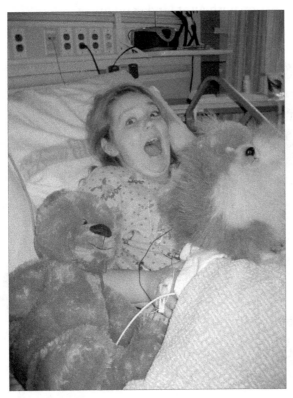

Hannah before her neurosurgery, Nov. 6, 2007

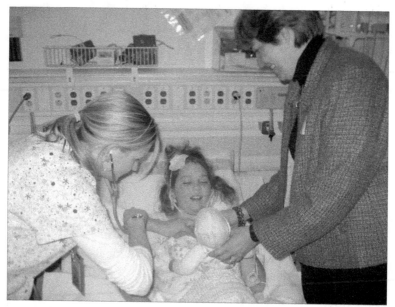

Hannah post-op with Aunt Linda and nurse

Greeting Buddy in the hospital parking garage as an inpatient

4

Complicated Gratitude

Following surgery, Hannah was a shell of her former self. After a couple days in the ICU she was moved back to the surgical floor. She was completely dependent on other people to help her do everything, including eating, dressing, and going to the bathroom. She could barely speak, and when she tried, she didn't make much sense. Having been an occupational therapist before I had children, I was trained in helping people overcome their disabilities and become more independent. I never thought I would be using those skills with my daughter.

Not only were we dealing with a very sick, weakened girl, we were also waiting to hear whether or not she had cancer. For five excruciating days we lived with the hope that her tumor was benign and that surgery was all she would need.

On Sunday afternoon, friends visited her hospital room. I appreciated the support, but honestly, it was difficult to entertain more than one or two close friends or family members while I was so worried about Hannah. And she wasn't in great shape to chat. She had a drainage tube coming out of the top of her head, she could barely talk, and she often fell asleep midsentence. In the midst of the visits, the surgeon called us with the pathology report. I left Hannah and walked into a conference room for privacy. The doctor told me that Hannah had anaplastic medulloblastoma.

My medical background sent me immediately into search mode as I tried to remember the meaning of the word *anaplastic*, knowing but not wanting to believe that it described an even more aggressive and lethal form of the tumor. Then my friend Sara appeared in the doorway. She always seemed to show up when I hadn't called but needed a friend. I shook my head and started to sob as she put her arms around me.

"Hannah has brain cancer. How could this tumor have been growing in her brain without us knowing it? How do we tell her? She's still not recovered from her surgery. She can barely speak, let alone think clearly. I can't imagine how she'll get through treatment too."

Sara sat with me until I had no more tears and nothing left to say.

After we met with Hannah's treatment team, we told our daughter that her tumor was cancerous and that she would need treatment. Whether her brain was still fuzzy from the surgery or she couldn't formulate the words, she didn't have much of a response. Gone was my eloquent daughter who was normally so in touch with her thoughts and feelings.

Hannah would have four weeks of recovery before starting chemotherapy and radiation. Given her extreme limitations, she was transferred to the rehab unit, where she received inpatient physical therapy, occupational therapy, speech therapy, and inpatient school tutoring to help her regain the skills she had lost from the surgery. The days were brutal. Hannah went from one therapy to another. I pushed her in a wheelchair to each session and then stayed to watch. It was hard to believe what I was seeing: my strong, coordinated, and athletic daughter now had trouble catching a ball that a two-year-old could manage.

At the end of each day, Hannah would sit in the bathtub down the hall from her room. It was quite an ordeal to set up the bath and get her in it, since she could do little to help herself. But the scented bubble bath and time alone with me helped her to relax. Back in her room, as Hannah fell into an exhausted sleep, I wrote in my journal and fielded phone calls from concerned friends. The mothers of Hannah's friends were the most worried, asking me questions about what to expect and when they could visit. It wasn't too long before I felt overwhelmed. I was still trying to wrap my head around Hannah's cancer and her disabilities; I couldn't take care of other women too.

While she was in the hospital, Hannah was showered with gifts. Stuffed animals, balloons, and cards occupied every available spot in her room. I loved that she was so beloved, but I hated what it was for. Each time a volunteer delivered a new gift bag, I felt a mix of joy and sadness. The gifts were reminders of how many people loved Hannah and also of how sick she was. When she was more recovered, I wheeled Hannah down to the hospital gift shop. The folks working the counter knew her name from all of the presents that had been purchased there. I wished she were famous for another reason.

While Hannah made slow but steady progress in rehab, Bill and I confronted another decision. Because Seattle Children's is part of the University of Washington and hence a teaching hospital and research center, Hannah was offered participation in a clinical study. But we wouldn't be able to choose the treatment—she would be randomly assigned to a protocol. The different protocols involved varying degrees of chemotherapy, radiation, and an adjunct medicine that was being tested for effectiveness as a supplement or alternative to harsher, more debilitating traditional chemotherapies for pediatric patients with high-risk medulloblastoma. More treatment could mean more side effects, but less treatment might not be as effective and therefore less of a cure.

I was leaning toward less treatment and fewer side effects, as Jeanette had conquered aggressive breast cancer through very alternative methods, declining chemotherapy even though it had been recommended. Bill, on the other hand, wanted to maximize Hannah's chances and hoped that she would receive all available treatments. For the first time, we weren't in agreement on what to do for Hannah.

We did agree that we were in one of the best hospitals in the country. And since Hannah was nine, she had a better chance of surviving this cancer than did kids half her age. More children survive medulloblastoma than don't. But hers was anaplastic, putting her in a higher risk category for survival with a worse prognosis. Given the odds, we rolled the dice and chose to have her participate in the study.

As I think back, I find it really astounding what we had to pray about—whether to hope for the most poison and the most invasive therapy or for the least poison and the least radiation to minimize her suffering and do the least harm. Neither guaranteed that Hannah would survive. In the end, she was randomly assigned to the arm of the study in which patients received *all* of the treatments—the research drug plus the most chemotherapy and the most radiation. When Cory, Hannah's nurse practitioner, showed up at Hannah's room with the news, I had just gotten out of the shower. My hair was dripping wet, but I felt such relief. I hugged Cory and said, "Thank goodness." After going back and forth with the decision, I felt hopeful for the first time in weeks. I thanked God that Hannah was in a place to get the best care possible, but I still wondered what the cost would be.

To get ready for radiation therapy, Hannah had to be fitted for a hard plastic mesh mask. Given her age, the staff in the radiation clinic wanted to sedate her for the procedure. I argued that she was mature and composed enough to handle the procedure without anesthesia. But I had no idea what I was talking about. First of all, Hannah wasn't her old self. She was an emotional and physical mess with limited mobility, poor control over her body, and difficulty expressing herself. She made it through the mask-making procedure without being sedated, but when I saw what she'd had to do, I was horrified. During the one-hour procedure, which must have been scary and claustrophobic for her, the mask was molded specifically to every contour of her face. It had small air holes, and when worn during radiation treatments it would be screwed to the table to immobilize her head. Many children need to be sedated for radiation treatments, but Hannah would manage to gut it out without anesthesia for the radiation sessions as well. I was relieved to see that a part of my tough daughter still remained.

The final step before treatment was the surgical implantation of a catheter port through which the chemotherapy would be adminis-tered. Although this was relatively minor surgery, nothing felt minor anymore. Hannah had to go without food beginning the night before surgery—not an easy thing for a girl on appetite-inducing steroids! And I was not looking forward to spending more time in the pre-op area as we had done before her neurosurgery. But, as it turned out, the procedure was uneventful.

In the midst of rehab and treatment preparations, Thanksgiving rolled around. I was disappointed but not surprised that we would be spending the holiday in the hospital. Family brought Thanksgiving to us: Linda and Claude, cousins, brothers, and Adam and his girlfriend all crowded around Hannah's hospital bed. The heavy doses of steroids that reduced inflammation in Hannah's brain caused serious mood swings as well as an insatiable appetite. Before dinner, we watched the movie *Rat Race* on the TV. Hannah randomly shouted out "Squirrel!" or "Cherry pie!" and then laughed hysterically. We tried to laugh along with her silliness and cravings, but an underlying tension and fear filled the room.

It seemed as if no one knew how to act or what to say around Hannah. Later in the evening, Ryan complained that we'd ruined Thanksgiving by having to spend it in the hospital. I bristled at his selfishness, but I eventually recognized his courage in speaking his truth. I felt torn between my own anger and fears around Hannah's future and my need to be present for my boys.

I had a lot of trepidations about Hannah's upcoming treatment. As much as I wanted to kill the cancer, I hated that poison was about to be poured into her body. And I wondered what radiation would do to her growing brain. *Will she be as smart? Will her personality change? How will her development be affected?* I kept my concerns away from Hannah. I had to be her primary support and cheerleader. I shared my fears with Bill and my friends, but with my daughter, I had to keep my composure. It wore me out.

Hannah handled the first week of chemotherapy and radiation with little pain and few side effects. Then she was cleared to go home from the hospital for the first time since she was diagnosed. But that hopeful homecoming was delayed when she began running a fever in the clinic. She couldn't be discharged if she was febrile, potentially coming down with something that her compromised immune system couldn't handle. Hannah, Bill, and I all cried. It had been a little over a month since she'd been home, and now it might be even longer. Fortunately, her fever subsided and by the end of the day she was allowed to leave.

We arrived home to a house fully decorated for Christmas. Friends had surprised us with colorful lights strung inside and out. A tree stood in the living room, waiting to be trimmed. Boxes of ornaments that classmates had made or purchased for Hannah were stacked around the tree. Hannah beamed with so much joy and so much love. I only felt a tinge of fear in the background, surrounded by this thoughtfulness. Home wasn't how we'd left it. But, filled with gratitude, I let out my breath for the first time in weeks.

Thanksgiving in Hannah's rehab room

With Dad in her rehab room

Unhappy camper in rehab

Lunch and a movie on a hospital pass
with cousin Caroline

5

The Longest Days and Nights

This Christmas respite was short-lived. During December, Hannah and I soaked up as much of home and family as we could get on the weekends. During the week, we moved into a hotel room close to the hospital, since she had daily treatments. Generous gifts from friends and coworkers made this convenience possible; commuting daily by ferry from home would have taken too much of Hannah's energy. We spent our days at the hospital in her various rehab therapies plus the chemo infusion, and then took a shuttle bus to the University of Washington Medical Center for the radiation session before returning to our hotel room. It was exhausting.

After a couple weeks of this routine, Hannah was suffering under its progressive toll. She lost her appetite and became increasingly weak and sick, despite the fact that she was on numerous medications to counteract her nausea—enough, it seemed, to take an elephant down. When I questioned the safety of so many narcotics in her system, Cory responded, "Have you met your daughter?"

We eventually had no choice but to agree to a feeding tube, which was inserted down her throat and attached to a backpack supplying liquid nutrition. She'd have to live with it for the next nine months. I hated it. At this point, though, it wasn't a choice. Hannah had quit eating and was barely drinking. Cory said, "I'm surprised she held out this long." I couldn't believe that my daughter with the normally voracious appetite was now being fed this way.

Between this new feeding contraption and the multitude of prescribed medications, Bill and I felt as if we needed nursing degrees to manage Hannah's care away from the hospital. We were at mile two of a marathon, and we didn't know how it would end.

Halfway through this intense regimen, Hannah had to reconcile with more loss. We were back at the hotel, getting ready to go to her radiation appointment. She started to brush her hair and noticed big blond clumps coming out in her hands. Her eyes got wide, and she yelped, "Mom, look at this." *Oh no,* I thought. *She's losing her hair.* We'd held onto a slim hope that Hannah would be one of the lucky ones who wouldn't go bald. "Let's just go to the hospital," she said, putting on a stiff upper lip.

The radiation clinic always had a basketful of knitted hats at the reception desk for the cancer patients. Before we walked back to the treatment room, Hannah grabbed a green, fuzzy hat and put it on. We both laughed. "It looks like you're a Chia head!" I said, trying to lighten up the situation.

Before Hannah lay down on the table underneath the radiation mask, the tech offered to take her picture with the new hat. Hannah had cut her long hair to shoulder length before starting treatment, knowing that she might lose it, and now it barely stuck out below the silly hat. Looking at the Polaroids, she declared, "I want to cut it all off. It's also really itchy." Here was my practical, no-nonsense girl.

After the treatment was finished, Hannah asked me to take her to the Great Clips across from our hotel. Fortunately, there was no wait. Hannah didn't have a chance to change her mind, and I had less time to fret about what was about to happen. As I helped her walk over to the stylist's chair, I remembered, months earlier, holding her in my lap and brushing my fingers through her long silky hair.

I had always loved Hannah's hair and wished mine were like it. Her blond hair was long, wavy, and soft; mine was brown, curly, and prone to tangles. I also loved to watch her style her hair—held up in a ponytail for soccer, plastered to her head with hairspray and bobby pins for dance recitals, adorned with barrettes or headbands for school or going out. My Leo daughter knew how to wear her mane. Now she had to learn "to put her pride in her pocket," as my friend Rae would say, as she lost it.

The stylist seemed a little flustered when she told him to "just shave it all off." But, a moment later, he recognized that he was looking at a young girl with cancer. The man was quiet as he buzzed Hannah's head, occasionally offering some nervous chatter. I had a lump in my throat, but to my surprise, neither one of us cried. I was grateful that it was over quickly and that Hannah hadn't hesitated. Here was my brave, beautiful daughter.

It wasn't the only time Hannah needed to be courageous. On an extended break from treatment just after Christmas, she became very sick with vomiting and diarrhea. After only a couple days at home, she sat in the bathtub, crying, "I just want to go back to the hospital. I don't want to be this sick at home."

I knew how bad Hannah—a girl who loved Christmas, not to mention the comforts of home—must have been feeling to ask to be taken back to the hospital. Cory had warned me that Hannah might need to be hospitalized. Part of me was relieved to have help with her physical care. Still, it was a sad New Year's Day when we returned to Children's to have Hannah admitted for the remainder of her treatment.

The next three weeks were a nightmare. Hannah finished the treatment as an inpatient, receiving around-the-clock nursing care for the multitude of secondary problems that arose. Despite this full-time nursing and medical support, I stayed at the hospital the whole time, sleeping in a chair bed in Hannah's room. I had thought it would be a respite to have professionals taking care of my daughter, but with Hannah so miserable, I found myself on the front lines of her care alongside the staff. I couldn't leave her.

It was hard for me to sleep at night. I lay awake, worrying about Hannah and listening to the cries of the other children on the floor. Hannah had to share a room with other sick kids and their families. It was not an environment for sleep or peace. One night, I listened to the comings and goings of a large family in the room next door, keeping vigil over their dying child.

Hannah's treatment whittled away at her strength and courage, not to mention her normally friendly demeanor, until she was nearly unrecognizable. Gone was my upbeat and friendly daughter, energetic and independent, excited about what the day had in store. Instead, I saw an angry, beaten-down, very sick girl with virtually no fight left in her. Most of her rehab therapies were on hold because she was too weak to participate in them. She screamed as if possessed when she got chemo at the infusion clinic. She refused to answer most people when they spoke to her, let alone look at them or offer her beautiful smile.

On one occasion, while receiving chemotherapy, Hannah noticed a baby, maybe nine months old, receiving chemo nearby. Hannah snapped, "Lucky baby. She's too young to remember all of this." True, but my former daughter who *loved* all babies would have seen her differently. She would have tried to talk to her or distract her from her treatment.

Instead, Hannah was only a witness to the horrible truth of cancer. And she wanted no part of it, either remaining silent or yelling at the nurses who administered to her. I wanted to yell, too: "THIS IS NOT MY DAUGHTER!"

Only one nurse seemed to recognize who my daughter was on the inside, the kid who was not only scared and angry but also sweet and lovable. Faith had a special way with Hannah, so we sought her out as often as we could. One of the oncology nurses' duties was accessing the port, which basically means stabbing the patient in the chest with a long, thick needle to reach the surgically embedded chemo port for treatment. Only Faith could access Hannah's port without eliciting bloodcurdling screams from her.

Hannah was often mean to her doctors. They were incredibly friendly and took as much time with her as they could, but Hannah wanted nothing to do with them. She especially hated waiting a long time to be seen. On one of her monthly checks, Dr. Olson, the head of her research study, was scheduled to examine Hannah but had been detained by a patient and their family in the ICU. When Jim entered the exam room, Hannah screamed at him, berating him for being so late. He finally had to leave the room; Hannah wouldn't allow him to complete the exam. I couldn't believe this ranting person was my daughter.

Many times throughout the day I felt like I should apologize for Hannah's actions. The kind, sensitive staff who could work with Hannah seemed few and far between, even those with hearts of gold, like Dr. Olson and Dr. Geyer, her primary oncologist. Everyone loved Hannah at home: her teachers, other parents, her friends. But now she railed against most everyone and everything having to do with her treatment. Part of me admired her fighting spirit. But it was a new experience for me, seeing Hannah this way. I couldn't wait for it to be over.

Each day felt like a year. I wished for a magic wand to transport Hannah and myself out of that hospital, out of that hell. We didn't belong there. I didn't want to get close to the staff or other patients and their families. Getting close meant identifying with the cancer. Hannah was my golden girl with a beautiful future, not a poster child or a disabled girl. So I hoped. I wanted to fast-forward time until this part of Hannah's life—and ours—was a distant memory.

During the last, worst weeks of Hannah's treatment, we counted down the remaining days on a whiteboard in her room. Each day that she completed her chemo and radiation felt like a victory that no one had the energy to celebrate.

After phase one of her treatment ended, Hannah had a month off to recover at home. That time flew by too quickly. Before I knew it, we were back in the hospital for the start of phase two.

The next seven months would involve monthly chemotherapy injections that were stronger and more toxic than the medicines administered in the first phase. Hannah, however, tolerated this cycle of treatments better than she had the harsh combination of radiation and chemotherapy in phase one. We were both relieved that the medicines didn't make her as sick. We found activities, like crafts and reading and movies, to pass the time for the five or so days we were in the hospital.

Most days were pretty peaceful, but some weren't. Some days, Hannah was hard to be around. She would be moody and irritable. I realized that some of Hannah's outbursts were a result of the boatload of medicines she had to consume daily. The steroids especially unleashed the devil in her.

One day, she was completely unreasonable. I had just gotten up from another restless night on the chair bed in her room. Her demands started quickly: "Mom, go to Starbucks and get me an almond hot chocolate with whipped cream. And hurry!"

When I returned with her drink, she took a sip, rolled her eyes, and snapped, "I didn't want that! Geez, can't you remember anything? And what took you so long?" The exchange escalated: "Why did you bring me these pajamas? Those are so ugly! Boy, I wish I'd gotten a mom with taste." The nurse in the room looked at me and shook her head slightly. "Hey kiddo, go easy on your mom. She's just trying to help."

Some of Hannah's comments were pretty mean; others were milder, but in my fragile, cancer-mom state it was easy to overreact. On that day, as Hannah continued to yell at me, I needed to put some space between us.

I left her room and walked the halls of the hospital, crying, unable to believe that this was our reality. I couldn't make eye contact with anyone I passed in the hallways or elevators. I ended up at Starbucks to get myself a drink. My coffee seemed to take forever to prepare. While I waited, I looked around at the hospital workers and visitors in the café. *Are they having as hard a day as I am? Did their screaming daughter just kick them out of a room? Has their world been turned upside down?*

Everyone else acted as if nothing was out of the ordinary. *Everything* felt out of the ordinary to me. The hospital staff would say, "Get used to your new normal," but I didn't want to get used to it. In between the fear and the anger and the sadness, I wondered if Hannah would ever return to a regular school, dance, or play soccer again. I wondered if her friends would abandon her if she couldn't keep up with them. I wanted our old life back.

Still, these months were easier than the past winter of radiation and chemo combined. A new countdown had begun. I couldn't wait for this phase to be over. The potent treatments consistently bottomed out her immune system, leaving her with zero white blood cells for protection. When that happened, we had to pack up and move into a hotel within a mile of the hospital. As soon as she spiked a small fever—which took anywhere from hours to days—we had to report to the emergency room. Hannah would be admitted to the hospital as a precaution, and we would wait for her blood counts to improve.

After every round, Hannah needed blood transfusions of platelets and red blood cells to help her recover. During one of these transfusions, Hannah had a bad reaction. Her blood pressure dropped, and the nurses came running. Fortunately, the reaction passed fairly quickly, but it was a reminder that no procedure on a child was risk-free.

Until Hannah got sick, I'd never personally known a child with cancer. My mind went to pictures from the St. Jude commercials: smiling, bald-headed kids accompanied by their parents and some celebrities in a pretty hospital. This picture was not our reality.

I'd known adult friends and family with cancer. I had watched survivors as they experienced nausea or fatigue or local soreness, but nothing like what I witnessed in Hannah's body or spirit. When Hannah developed brain cancer, she essentially sustained a traumatic brain injury. Her surgery likely took out healthy brain tissue, leaving her with a multitude of physical, emotional, and cognitive disabilities. Radiation and chemotherapy further impeded her growth and normal development.

I told whoever would listen, "Hannah's been through hell."

With a new feeding tube and a bald Dad

At a low point during intense treatment

Exhausted and finally home after phase one

6

Setback

It was a beautiful spring day in April; apple trees blossomed, and lilacs perfumed the air. I dreaded having to leave home and go back to Children's Hospital, but we had no choice. Hannah's feeding tube had become accidentally dislodged when she was eating some Cheetos, and it needed to be immediately replaced. We hoped it would be a quick trip to the outpatient clinic.

I started to cry when Cory showed us the X-ray taken to ensure the feeding tube was in the correct position. It showed air in Hannah's intestines, a problem that could lead to rupture and a potentially life-threatening condition. "Unfortunately, this can happen with our kids after months of chemotherapy," Cory said, and explained that Hannah would have to be hospitalized.

"You're kidding, right?" I didn't want to believe it. Hannah had just gotten out of the hospital only a few days earlier, after one of her monthly post-chemo nosedives to zero white blood cells, a fever, and no immunity.

"No, I'm serious," Cory said. "We need to keep her here and monitor her in case she needs emergency surgery."

Hannah moaned and groaned as we walked into her hospital room, back on the surgical floor that we thought we'd never have to see again. I had wanted to have a parade when we'd left months earlier. At least this time Hannah would have a private room with her own bathroom. But then the nurse came in to tell her she couldn't eat or drink anything. The doctors had ordered that she be placed on IV fluids and nutrition to allow her gut to rest.

"Great! Just what I needed," Hannah snarked, and then she started to cry. "Well, at least I get you all to myself!" she said to me. She soon settled into making the best of the bad situation.

She wasn't in any pain, even though her stomach threatened to erupt at any moment. Forced to be quiet and rest, she found things to keep herself busy. Friends often brought her crafts to occupy her in the hospital, so during this stay she painted a jewelry box and a birdhouse in bright neon colors.

Practically anyone who visited Hannah also had to play at least one game of Uno. She considered herself a card shark. "You're goin' down! There's a new Uno champion in town today!" she teased her speech therapist.

Another one of her favorite distractions was having Nancy Drew books read to her. The surgery had interfered with her vision, making reading on her own slow and tiresome. I was her chosen reader. Hannah and I made it through a half dozen mysteries during that stay.

At night, with the lights turned down low and Hannah asleep, it was impossible for me to read anything. I wrote in my journal so I wouldn't forget what had happened that day. Sometimes I opened up my computer to update CaringBridge, an online journal I was keeping to inform everyone in our community of Hannah's progress.

In one entry I wrote, "Hannah's handling this turn of events pretty well, although she's had some MAD, screaming, uncooperative moments in the last 24 hours. I am just sad for her. And for us."

I also watched a lot of movies on my computer, trying to put my mind someplace else. I wanted to forget where we really were.

During the day, while Hannah entertained herself in bed with crafts and books and visitors, I found myself overwhelmed with fear. When I could, I left her room and paced the hallways, round and round the nurses' station. To keep contact with the outside world, I'd call friends and family on my cell phone.

One day, just as I hung up with Bill, Cory called to check in. I pummeled her with questions she didn't have answers to. I wanted to know when Hannah would be okay, when we could leave the hospital, and why this had happened to her. I told Cory that ten years earlier my mom had died in the ICU after having emergency abdominal surgery.

I had sat at Mom's hospital bedside for hours at a time as she slept. Watching the monitors. Listening to the beeps of IVs needing changing. Hearing the alarms when there was a problem with her ventilator. Watching her code and being kicked out of her room so the staff could try to resuscitate her. Flying back to Cincinnati repeatedly because she likely wouldn't live through the night. Being with Mom in her final days. Saying goodbye.

After I got off the phone with Cory, I had to pull myself together before I could go back into Hannah's room. I found myself praying. I pleaded and wailed to God. "She's had enough! So have I! Please spare her from having another major surgery. Make the problem go away!"

I couldn't bear the thought that Hannah's fate would be the same as Mom's. And I couldn't stay in this agonized state as the days wore on and Hannah's condition didn't change. I needed a distraction. Hannah was comfortable and having fun. Why couldn't I? Bill's and my anniversary had just passed, uncelebrated. So we decided to go out to dinner.

We arranged for a family friend to stay with Hannah in the hospital while we were gone. Bill and I had a lovely meal in a small, quiet café. With soft music, a glass or two of wine, and adult conversation, I started to feel better. I definitely needed to get some separation from the continuous days and nights at the hospital, hovering over Hannah for any sign of trouble.

In the following days, I took more breaks and gave myself more time-outs. As I relaxed, so did Hannah's gut. After repeated daily X-rays, the doctors decided that the air in her intestines was leaving. She wouldn't need surgery, thank God. We had escaped this time. And, finally, Hannah could begin to drink again, starting with clear liquids.

When the tray arrived, Hannah called Bill on the phone and said, "I'm having chicken broth for dinner!" And then, with a big old smile, "I'm livin' the dream!" My daughter was a bowl-half-full kind of girl. I'm still learning how not to be a glass-half-empty mom.

7

Recovery

Hannah's intestinal problem was the last major complication of her treatment. She and I got into a groove with her monthly inpatient chemo infusions, followed by hospital stays when her blood counts bottomed out. Her steroid-driven outbursts were less frequent—either that or I had grown accustomed to dealing with them. The predictable routine of treatment was easier to manage than the unknown, but it wasn't where either one of us wanted to be.

During her recovery time at home, Hannah missed her large circle of girlfriends, so she leaned on family, primarily Bill and me, for support. She had never been very close to her two older brothers. Before she got sick, Hannah had never seemed to need her brothers, and Ryan and Andrew—so close to each other—didn't pay a lot of attention to her either. People used to ask me if they treated their little sister like a princess. I'd laugh and say, "No, it's more like boot camp." Her athletic brothers had encouraged her to be tough, and she seemed to thrive on the challenge and her independence. But when Hannah got sick, she looked at them differently.

One day, it occurred to Hannah that she needed her brothers. She lay crying on the couch, telling me, "I only want them to love me." I called Ryan and Andrew in to talk with her. Hannah kept her head down and had trouble making eye contact with the boys. Trying to compose herself, she asked, "Can I have a hug?"

The brothers were pretty speechless over her new request. Hannah had never asked for much of anything from them before, let alone a hug or to say that they loved her. I was delighted that Hannah was speaking up for what she needed. When I nudged them, Ryan and Andrew gave their sister a hug and said, "I love you." It was a nice mom moment. And then they went back to their video games.

From the day Hannah was born, I'd had an intuition that she would heal our family in some way. Never in a million years did I think she would have a life-threatening illness, but it drew people close to her. I couldn't tell at the time if this particular interaction would have a transforming effect on Ryan and Andrew. I was just grateful for their new connections.

Even though Hannah seldom saw her oldest brother, Adam, she didn't have to work as hard to be close to him. In May, he and his girl-friend, Alexis, were graduating from law school in Chicago. The timing was terrible: the ceremony coincided with one of Hannah's monthly treatments. She worried the week before if she would be well enough to go. I doubted that her treatment team would give her the green light, given her compromised immune system, but I had trouble telling her a definitive no. I hated to give Hannah one more disappointment.

When I finally told her it wouldn't be possible to make the trip, she had a mixed reaction. She cried quietly at the news, but she also seemed somewhat relieved. I encouraged her to call Adam, knowing he would make her feel better. When she got off the phone, she said, "At least I won't be holding people back."

With her limited mobility and endurance, she had talked to me about how hard it was to keep up with other people and how she hated being a "weight." I told her, "Maybe we can take a trip to New York City to see Adam next year, when you're done with treatment and feeling better." Her eyes lit up. I was relieved that she wouldn't have to carry the burden in Chicago, but I was sad for her too. I was sad for how much she and I had missed out on.

As the school year came to an end, Hannah was able to participate in some fourth grade rites of passage. Her class at school created a role for her in the spring play. The music teacher made her an old-fashioned costume that included a big floppy hat. Hannah sat on a stool behind a flower stand so classmates could include her and she wouldn't have to walk around. But she still needed a walker to get positioned on the stage. And she still had a feeding tube that was hard to disguise.

I was grateful for their efforts to include my daughter, but it was tough to see her on stage as less than her formerly strong self. I was anxious for her and for others in the community who hadn't seen Hannah since she'd been sick, but she didn't hesitate to accept her role.

Just in time for the play, Hannah asked for a wig. At the store, we settled on a shoulder-length blond wig that barely resembled her original hair. For a short time it seemed to give her new confidence, but within weeks, she put the wig on a stand in her bedroom and never wore it again. I was just as glad when she gave it up. Wearing a wig was pretending she was normal when she wasn't.

A few weeks after the school play, Hannah participated in part of the fourth grade's outdoor school program, held at an environmental facility on the island. Students and parent volunteers stayed in cabins on the property and took part in outdoor activities during the day. Hannah, before cancer, would have loved this camping week with her friends. But in her current condition she couldn't fully engage. At first we planned to just join the class for a dinner, but Hannah's friends swept her up and insisted that she spend the night in their cabin.

"Please, can I stay?" Hannah asked with excitement.

"Of course," I said.

I was thrilled that she could have a sleepover with her buddies, without me present for a change. But she was severely limited in what she could do. After supper, a friend and I pushed her around the grounds in a wheelchair before I left for the night. Hannah seemed happy when I picked her up the next morning, but leaving before the camp was over was another reminder of her limited capacity.

Just when I was feeling discouraged about Hannah's diminished health or functioning, we would get a reminder of her progress. Chief among those were the clean MRIs she'd received every two months since the day she was diagnosed. Hearing that she was cancer-free was a huge relief, but waiting for those results never got easier.

Hannah was more frustrated with her lack of growth. During every clinic checkup, she groaned every time the scale showed that she was no taller. Height was the least of our concerns, but Hannah complained about her short stature, knowing full well she was part of a tall family and all the grown children of her generation reached at least six feet. I reminded myself that she could take growth or fertility hormones in the future to correct what her body wasn't doing naturally. The most important thing was that she had survived.

In celebration of Hannah's survival, I wanted to participate in the American Cancer Society's Relay for Life on the island that summer. Hannah wanted to do the survivor's victory lap. As Bill and I supported her on both sides, we took a very slow walk around the track, with Ryan and Andrew meeting us halfway to the finish. I cried the whole way around. I cried for Hannah, for us, and for those who had not survived. I was also reminded of the races I'd participated in over the years. I felt the familiar adrenaline rush from the upbeat music and the cheering crowd, but this was like no race I had ever run before. One lap had felt like an eternity, but now we were so close to the finish line.

By August Hannah was done with phase two of treatment. That meant no more hospitalizations, no more urgent trips to the emergency room, no more chemo or blood transfusions, no more missed life. Now the real recovery could begin.

We celebrated Hannah's birthday and the end of treatment with a trip to a day spa. Aunt Linda, cousin Caroline, and I accompanied her for the day of pampering. Hannah loved it. I saw the spa workers' stares as they noticed Hannah's bald head and feeding tube. But this time I didn't mind. I told myself that soon they would be things of the past. The four of us made a pact that we would make this spa day an annual girls' and moms' treat.

Feeling better by the day, Hannah wanted to express her gratitude to everyone who had supported her. She started with writing an email to Grace Church's priest and our friend, Bill Harper, on August 11, 2008. As she instructed, we stood with her in a circle at Grace while Bill read her email:

> Hi Bill,
>
> It's Hannah. This morning I thought that we should pay a visit to church. I think we have a lot of thanking to do. I was wondering if you could speak in front of church to help me say thank you? I was thinking of saying something like this . . .
>
> Thank you for everyone for being so supportive, for giving me beautiful cards almost every day. Thank you for giving me gifts and stuffed animals. But most of all even though I didn't see very much people you still prayed for me in church and on the website. Also thanks to God that I wasn't very sick at the end, and I'm so happy and glad that I stayed alive.
>
> I just wanted to take this time to thank everybody.
>
> When you speak I want my whole family up there with you.
>
> Hope we can make this happen.
>
> Love,
>
> Hannah

It was an emotional moment, standing in the circle with Hannah and our family as Bill read her letter. I was so grateful that my daughter had "stayed alive," as she said. Fear and anxiety were finally leaving me. I felt nothing but hope for our future.

Forward progress continued into the fall. Before school started, Hannah finally had her feeding tube removed after nine long months, and we took a celebratory family vacation to Victoria, BC, a favorite place for Hannah and her close friend and "big sister," Alli. The girls had taken a trip there on their own just months before Hannah was diagnosed.

Now, a year later, she still used a wheelchair because she was not yet able to walk very far. The chair definitely limited our activities. And even though she had gotten rid of the feeding tube, her bald head and limited mobility drew looks when we were out and about. Despite the hardships, the trip helped me feel that our lives were starting up again.

Back home, as the new school year began, I watched my daughter slowly reappear. With the help and support of her friends, teachers, and counselors, she started to thrive in the fifth grade despite her disabilities. Hannah's only expressed concern about going back to school was how other people would treat her and see her. She wondered, "What are the kids gonna say about my bald head and the fact that I walk funny?"

Hannah no longer needed the wheelchair by this point, but she still used a walker to get around. I worried that she would fall or not have the stamina to get through a day. I wasn't really concerned that kids would tease her. As far as I knew, they didn't, and she soon blended back in with her peers.

Hannah attended school full days and did her homework as soon as she walked in the door. It was a struggle for her to meet her former standards, given her low endurance and decreased ability to focus. She had also lost the ability to write with her dominant right hand. Completing her work with her left hand required a lot of effort and time. I'd been used to Hannah not needing help with homework. Now I offered to help her, but she often refused. When I couldn't get her to budge and take a break, I began to lose patience. It helped that we asked our friend Maureen, a teacher, to tutor Hannah. I slowly realized that I would need to rely on others to help Hannah at home, just as the many nurses, therapists, and doctors had helped her at the hospital. I couldn't be her sole support.

Besides schoolwork, Hannah's days were filled with lots of activities. Physical and occupational therapy were built into her day by thoughtful therapists who included her friends in her rehab activities at recess. Sue, the physical therapist, got Hannah involved in an adaptive soccer program. This version of the sport was a far cry from what we'd been used to, but I told myself it was a start. She joined the kids' choir at Grace Church at the encouragement of its music director, Ann, who'd taken a special interest in Hannah. We even fit in private swimming lessons in a warm pool. When she wasn't working or rehabbing, Hannah made time for her girlfriends. I loved having her friends back at the house again, laughing and playing. Everything seemed to be happening for Hannah's recovery.

One procedure was still needed to put Hannah's world as a cancer patient behind her. I was anxious for the removal of her chemo port, one of the last remnants of her treatment. This procedure involved outpatient surgery. After being away from the hospital for a couple months, I found it a shock to go from the "hurry up" world of home and school to the "slow down and wait" world of the hospital—not to mention all the bad memories the place held.

In the operating prep room, we waited for hours due to backed-up cases. By the time they were ready for her, Hannah was an emotional wreck. This minor procedure was one too many for her. Fortunately, a kind anesthesiologist allowed me to gown up from head to toe and stay with my daughter as they wheeled her to surgery. I was surprisingly calm and not a sobbing mess as we walked into the brightly lit surgical room. It was comforting to watch Hannah go from crying to laughing to telling me she loved me as she went to sleep.

With Hannah on the road to wellness, I finally had time to look at something besides my needy daughter. Our family needed to recover as much as Hannah did. We seemed to be in some sort of post-traumatic, dysfunctional family funk. Tempers were short. Communication was lacking. Life was too busy. In the previous year I'd gotten used to taking care of only one child at a time. Now I faced the struggles and desires of three children and a husband trying to find their way back into a so-called normal family.

When friends asked me how I was doing, I would sometimes say, "I'm waiting for the second-string parents to show up." I wished for grandparents to take over. I wanted *anyone* to move in and tell us what to do to manage our lives. I had been told that this process was to be expected—recovering the family—but it was no fun. I trusted we would survive this period. And I reminded myself that we had everything to be thankful for—Hannah's survival.

In November we celebrated the one-year anniversary of her diagnosis and surgery. The MRIs told us she was cancer-free. She was thriving and getting her life back. We all had much to be grateful for on Thanksgiving. Miles apart from the crazy holiday dinner at the hospital the year before, we welcomed Linda, Claude, and the cousins to our home for the day. Hannah helped me make dinner and set the fancy table. We played games and talked and laughed. I couldn't have been happier.

The good mood continued into the holiday season. Again, in contrast to the hellish Christmas the year before, Hannah accepted every invitation she could. Alli treated Hannah to dinner out in Seattle, followed by a surprise backstage tour of Pacific Northwest Ballet's *The Nutcracker*. Alli had performed in the local production from the time she was a young girl, so it was a special experience. Hannah dreamed of following in her big sister's dancing shoes. During the tour she received Clara's pointe shoes from the performance. Hannah glowed as she told me about it.

The celebration continued into the new year, when Hannah finally finished her research drug. Other than giving her very dry skin, the medicine had come with few side effects. Nothing could have made us happier than throwing that empty drug package away. Hannah was officially off treatment. With another clean MRI scan, we had everything to look forward to, including a trip to New York City to visit Adam. After so much had been denied or put on hold, we felt we finally had our lives back.

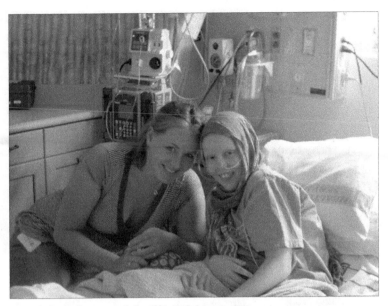

Receiving chemo with Alli visiting

Sporting her new walker

With Courtney at the spring play

Outdoor school sleepover

Vacation in Victoria, British Columbia

One year cancer-free with Jeanette

With Alli backstage at *The Nutcracker*

8

The Time of Our Lives

At the end of March 2009, we took our promised trip to New York City for spring break. We were ready to celebrate that Hannah had finished her treatment. Adam and Alexis were now living together in Manhattan, working in law firms. Hannah hadn't seen her older brother since Thanksgiving 2007, and she was excited—"I can't wait for Adam to see how good I look now!" We were all glad to take a vacation from everything cancer-related.

When we arrived in the city, it was like stepping into a whole other world. We stayed in a big hotel in Times Square. Getting out of the cab felt like the scene in the movie *Enchanted* where the princess is thrown from her animated country life into a bustling real-world city of big lights and tall buildings. I had last seen that film when Hannah was newly recovering from brain surgery. She had gotten a pass to leave the hospital for the first time, so Bill and I, with her cousin Caroline, took her out to dinner and the movie. At the time, I was still in disbelief that we had entered this alternate world of childhood cancer. The movie was a welcome escape. Now, in the Big Apple, we had escaped the cancer life we'd known and wanted to forget.

It wasn't hard to find things to do. Our kids had never been to New York, so we packed in a lot of sightseeing. We saw the highlights—the Empire State Building, the Statue of Liberty, Central Park, and the Museum of Natural History. We endured long lines and a lot of walking, which at times was tough for Hannah's reduced endurance. But she never quit. When she got too tired, Bill or Adam carried her.

Hannah and I also tagged along as Bill and Adam went ring shopping. Adam was getting ready to propose marriage to Alexis. Hannah couldn't wait for the proposal. My shopping girl loved the opportunity to look at diamonds and fancy jewelry and to dream of a wedding. Finally, we all had something to look forward to.

By far the best part of the trip for Hannah and me was seeing the Broadway musical *Mamma Mia!* We loved the movie. We loved the singing, the dancing, the love stories. We'd probably seen it at least ten times, in the theater and at home. By the time we saw the show live, we knew all the songs by heart. Bill had treated us to orchestra seats, very close to the stage. Hannah wore a fancy shirt, leggings, and makeup. I wore the nicest clothes I'd brought plus my mom's pearls. Before the show started, Hannah giggled and squealed with excitement. She sat on the edge of her seat through the whole performance, mouthing along with the songs. I smiled and sang through the whole show, crying happy tears during the encore because Hannah and I were finally doing something we both loved. The only time I felt a little sad or self-conscious was when other patrons stared at Hannah's very short chemo hair. The scar on her chest from the chemo port was also visible, but she didn't seem to mind. I don't think she noticed people looking; if she had, she would have said something like "I wish people would get a life and quit staring!"

When we left the theater, Hannah was exhausted and asked to take a bicycle taxi back to the hotel. Once again, some people stared as we were driven through the streets. I thought about how the old Hannah could have walked miles back to the hotel. It was a painful reminder of a chapter I hoped and believed was in the past.

I was trying to forget all that we had been through since her diagnosis. On this day, leaving the musical, I was happy, doing something with my daughter that we both loved. But the joy was tinged with fear. Most of me believed I no longer had to fear for her life. She was done with treatment and could focus on getting back to what regular ten-year-olds loved to do. Hannah had spent too much of the past months sacrificing events and activities because she was too sick or too compromised. Now we could both look forward to living again.

Hannah loved music. She was my dancing queen. For as long as I can remember, she was always singing, dancing, or playing music. At age three she had started classes at Bainbridge Dance Center. One of her teachers knew how much dance meant to Hannah. She also understood that Hannah couldn't keep up with her peers in regular classes after she had gone through treatment. Graciously, BryAnn offered private lessons, at no charge, so that Hannah could enjoy the rehearsal space at the dance center and learn dance routines. BryAnn and I danced right along with Hannah so she would feel part of a group. It wasn't like the old days of tap and ballet classes with her friends, but it was something.

When our vacation ended, Hannah was excited to get back home and resume her dancing. I was excited to leave the big city and return to our "new normal" life on Bainbridge—dance lessons, school drop-offs and pickups, homework, nightly dinners. The trip had been a welcome respite for Hannah and our whole family.

Hannah being carried by Bill and Adam

At *Mamma Mia!*

Dinner out with Adam and Alexis

9

Relapse

We had just returned from our fabulous trip to New York. Hannah and her brothers were back in school. The weather was warming up, turning the Pacific Northwest into a flower garden. And I was appreciating not only our island home but also Hannah's improving health. I wanted nothing more than to put the past twenty months behind us.

Two weeks after we got back, on an especially warm spring day, Hannah and I got in the car and took the ferry to Seattle for her routine MRI scan at Children's. Bill was already in the city for a different meeting. When we picked him up downtown, everyone was in a good mood. On the way to the hospital, we talked about where we would go for lunch after the scan and where we would go for a summer vacation. It seemed like nothing but sunny skies ahead for us.

I had given Hannah a sedative on the boat—not for the scan but for the necessary IV poke prior to the MRI. If the nurse didn't access a vein on the first try, Hannah would squirm and cry in fear of the needle. It was one of the few times in all of her hospital trials that she acted more like a little kid. On this day, the nurse hit her mark the first time.

After the IV prep, I walked back through the secure double doors to the dark MRI room with a groggy, slightly stumbling Hannah. I helped her onto the table and covered her with a warm blanket, as was our normal routine. She had her headphones on and her Kelly Clarkson music cued up for the test. I sat in the chair at the foot of the table, staring at a pile of magazines. Before the loud pounding of the MRI machine began,

I put in the rubber earplugs the staff had given me to drown out the noise. I settled into the chair, not particularly worried about Hannah because she found these tests relaxing.

Thirty minutes later, a radiation tech walked back into the room. "Is the test finished already?" I asked. "No," she answered. "Hannah needs to come with me next door to another MRI machine." I followed behind, mouth suddenly dry and heart pounding in my chest. The only other time they'd had to use this second machine was on the day of the diagnosis, when they needed spinal films, not just images of her brain. I tried to take deep breaths and calm myself, but I was already on high alert. I felt the same tingling sensation in the back of my head I'd experienced when Hannah's neurosurgery was over. My brain was bursting with questions: *What does this new scan procedure mean? Is something wrong? Has the radiologist seen something on the first pictures? Is Hannah's cancer back?*

Hannah seemed unfazed by the added procedure. Maybe she was still in a relaxed state from the sedative, but she didn't ask any questions about why they'd taken more pictures.

I didn't say anything to Hannah or Bill about my concerns during our lunch at our normal Italian place. But I couldn't eat. I didn't normally order wine for lunch, but this time I did, trying to calm myself down. My mind was racing with fear.

Back at the clinic after lunch, I saw it on Dr. Geyer's face as soon as he walked into the exam room. "Folks, we have a problem," he said.

As Dr. Geyer showed us new tumors on the screen, Hannah was silent. Bill and I mumbled through some questions, but I found myself in the same stunned state of mind as when we first heard that Hannah had a brain tumor. I was terrified of hearing the new prognosis, but I had to know the truth.

I pulled Dr. Geyer and Cory into the adjacent exam room, away from Hannah's ears. "Are you telling me my daughter is going to die? How much time does she have?"

They told me one to two years.

I shook my head. "That's impossible. She seems fine!"

What followed was a blur. Once again, I couldn't stop crying. *My daughter is going to die?* I repeated to myself. I sat with Hannah in the back seat of the car on the way home. She called a couple of her girlfriends on the ride and calmly told them that her cancer was back. Maybe Hannah was in shock, or in need of connection with her friends, but she sounded more like she was giving a news report and not the dire prognosis that it was. I couldn't imagine what those friends or their mothers had to deal with for the rest of the day.

The next day, Bill and I dropped Hannah off in Seattle with Alli so that we could meet with her treatment team to discuss the options. Still in shock and feeling utterly defeated, I sat on the floor of the conference room with my back up against the wall. Her team ran through the gamut of choices: Hannah could repeat what she'd already been through—surgery, chemotherapy, and radiation—or she could try a different, possibly more tolerable oral chemotherapy.

We once again faced nightmare choices: to be more aggressive to maybe get rid of the cancer or to be more humane and allow Hannah to continue living her life at home, at school, and with her friends. Cory summed up our choices: "You're in hell. Hell with decisions."

We ultimately decided to ask Hannah what she wanted to do. On the ferry ride home, she seemed relieved to hear that she could choose a treatment that wouldn't mean more brutal protocols requiring hospitalization and that might let her keep her hair. Of course, she didn't fully understand that there was no treatment that would stop the cancer's progression. We couldn't tell her that. So it seemed pointless to try to persuade her to opt for any of the more aggressive choices.

Despite her hopefulness that she could fight the cancer again, my smart girl knew what she was up against. The day before, when we'd come home from that fateful MRI, Hannah had asked us point-blank if she was going to die. We'd been counseled by the Children's staff to not answer this question directly to keep some hope alive. I tried to dodge her pleas, but Hannah persisted: "Am I going to die? Am I going to die?

Am I going to die? I don't want to leave you! I wanted to be a mother. Is heaven like my life here? Dear God, please don't let me die from this disease. I don't know how I could leave my family."

Hannah had a warrior spirit. During her cancer treatment, she had discovered this quote from Buddhist teacher, Jack Kornfield: "To open deeply, as genuine spiritual life requires, we need tremendous courage and strength, a kind of warrior spirit. But the place for this warrior strength is in the heart." With the return of her cancer, these words became her mantra. She had a great spirit, a great heart, and great courage.

Hannah was a fighter, in a vital, positive, life-affirming way, especially before she got sick. Throughout her life she was more hopeful than pessimistic, more cooperative than competitive, more of a giver than a taker, more loving than oppositional, more friendly than aloof, more funny than sarcastic, more grateful than arrogant, more selfless than selfish. Some of these attributes waned as the cancer and its treatment progressed. But in her heart she was a spiritual warrior.

During the first rounds of her treatment, Hannah had been too disabled and too weak to put up much of a fight. She accepted the treatments, interspersing them with occasional outbursts of anger, sadness, and defeat. It was quite an ordeal, watching this strong-willed girl surrender to what had to be done. As the treatments became more bearable, she gradually became more herself again—vocal, funny, and assertive.

When her cancer returned, Hannah actively took up the fight to save her life. "I'm going to kick cancer in the butt!" she said through tears. In addition to the new chemotherapy, Hannah added a number of holistic modalities to her treatment arsenal: nutritional supplements, exercise, sound therapy, yoga, and meditation. The yoga and meditation practices seemed to bring her to a new level of peace and surrender to whatever the future might hold. I would watch her relax completely in Savasana (also called Corpse Pose) at the end of a yoga session with Sue. I believe that in these still and quiet times she was in touch with her infinite soul, the part of her that the cancer could not touch. The part of her that she would take with her after her last breath.

I admired Hannah's new strength and determination, but I was reeling with the knowledge that my daughter would die. I didn't know how I would live with myself once she was gone, knowing that I had willed her into creation. After my mom's excruciating illness, I had known in my heart of hearts that I wanted to have a girl—one who could share with me her life, her children, and a closeness that I hadn't had with my own mom. I guess God had another plan.

After we met with the care team and decided on the easier course of treatment, a number of people came to the house to check on us. My brother was one of the first to show up. He didn't say a word but let out long sighs. Maybe he didn't know what to say. I really didn't know what Claude was thinking, but I wished that he could have said or done something to make me feel better. I later learned that Hannah's relapse was a turning point for him.

Close friends who could tolerate my sadness showed up to cry with me and offer hugs and words of encouragement. Sara, who had been with me just after we'd learned that Hannah had cancer, sat and just listened. As I cried on her shoulder, I said, "I don't want to be the grieving mom. I don't want to be the expert on death and dying. I can't imagine my life without Hannah."

If I'd known that a malignant tumor would randomly plant itself in my daughter's brain while she was in utero, I wouldn't have willed her into being. While she had encountered some unusual health obstacles when she was young, for nine years there had been no signs that she wouldn't be here very long. A kidney infection when she was just a year old led to a CT scan at the hospital. An abnormal heart sound detected when she was seven led to a cardiogram in a clinic and the diagnosis of an "innocent," nonthreatening heart murmur. Should I have known that these unusual ailments were omens of something more deadly to come? I didn't believe so at the time. What I saw was my healthy, active daughter growing up and thriving.

But Hannah wouldn't grow up. She would never fall in love, graduate from high school, go to college, get married, or have her own children, which she seemed to want so badly even from an early age. Hannah was such a natural caretaker. She loved playing mom to her friends, her pets, and her baby dolls. How could she not be there for me, to take care of me as I had envisioned?

How selfish was that? I was so angry that I would become the bereaved mother and the counselor to other grieving women. THIS WAS NOT WHAT I HAD PLANNED.

Why did Hannah have to die? Why do children have to die? In her book *On Life after Death*, Dr. Elisabeth Kübler-Ross posed this question and said: "The answer is quite simple. They have learned in a very short period what one has to learn, which could be different things for different people. There is one thing everybody has to learn before he can return from where he came, and that is unconditional love. If you have learned and practiced this, you have mastered the greatest lesson of all." No big surprise that Hannah had mastered loving, but small comfort to believe that she had learned her lesson and no longer needed to be here.

For a long time after her relapse, I was consumed with guilt that I had brought this child into the world only to have her in agony for a good portion of it. How selfish was I that I wanted to produce a child, a girl, to take care of me in my old age? Of course, I knew in the back of my mind that her soul had other ideas, lessons to learn other than taking care of her mother. I just didn't want it to be true.

Bill with a determined Hannah
doing yoga

My girl

Our family at cousin Annie's graduation, June 2009

10

A Wish

I t was hard to believe that Hannah's cancer was back, and I absolutely refused to accept that she would die. She didn't seem sick. She had no symptoms. It wasn't like the beginning of her illness, when she had severe headaches and back pain. Still, I felt an urgency to make plans for what Hannah wanted to do with the time she had left. Her treatment team was telling us to not waste time in granting any of her wishes.

Hannah qualified for a Make-A-Wish trip. Her first wish was to meet her favorite singer, pop star Ashley Tisdale, of the *High School Musical* movies. When *High School Musical 2* came out in the fall of 2008, after her cancer treatment had ended, Hannah made a night of it with her best girlfriends. At that time, there was every hope in the world that cancer would just be a blip in Hannah's life. But now we faced the fact that she would die.

When the Make-A-Wish Foundation couldn't arrange a meeting with Ashley, one of Bill's real estate colleagues worked some magic to set up a meeting with her. In preparation for the trip, Hannah wrote this letter:

Dear Ashley,

Hi. My name is Hannah Hunt. I'm ten years old. I live in Seattle, WA on beautiful Bainbridge Island. I was diagnosed November 5th, 2007 with a Brain Tumor and had treatment ever since.

I am very outgoing, fun to be with. I have a good sense of humor and like to laugh a LOT! I have tons of friends. I ABSOLUTELY LOVE DANCING!!! Before I got diagnosed, dancing and friends were my life. And to be pulled away from that is so hard. I'm a great student. My classmates have been so supportive through all of this! They're really welcoming when I come in and visit! I volunteer in younger classrooms to read or help out. I'm very responsible and my parents agree.

I am so grateful that I get a make a wish. It used to be only for kids who were going to not make it. But now any kid with a life-threatening illness can have a make a wish. I chose you because I really feel like I can look up to you for advice. You are an inspiration to me because I love, love, love your music and your dancing. I REALLY want to see your outfits in person, plus, I think you're extremely pretty. You're like a whole package deal!!!

Having cancer doesn't separate me from the outside world. My friends do not care what I look like on the outside. It's the inside that counts.

Love,

Hannah

A month after her relapse, Hannah and I flew to Los Angeles. We stayed at the famed Century Plaza Hotel, across the street from where we would meet Ashley. It was thrilling to walk into the two-story lobby with midcentury chandeliers hanging from the tall ceilings. In this kind of ambience, I almost forgot why we were there—to grant a last wish. After checking into our room, Hannah and I went outside, sat by the pool, and ordered lemonade and French fries. I took a lot of pictures of Hannah and of the two of us in chaise lounge chairs, trying to capture our time together. *How many more trips like this will we get to have?*

Hannah couldn't tolerate the Southern California sun for long, so we left the pool and walked across the street to a shopping mall, a normally favorite place for my daughter to explore. But Hannah was running low on energy, so we found ourselves sitting at the makeup counter at Sephora. Hannah loved getting makeovers. She was already losing her hair from the new oral chemo drug. With bald patches on her head, she didn't look as good as she would have liked for meeting her idol, but she didn't say a word about her appearance.

The next day, we ordered room service for breakfast, one of our favorite things to do. In an excited mood, Hannah dressed quickly in a carefully chosen outfit. Before I knew it, we were walking across the street to meet Ashley at her agent's office. At Creative Artists Agency, we were escorted into a large, modern reception room. I did not expect what happened next. When Ashley appeared, my normally social, talkative daughter was suddenly tongue-tied. I tried my best to keep the conversation going. Ashley was kind and as sweet as could be, but Hannah could hardly look at her. When it came time to take pictures and say goodbye, Hannah's bright, warm smile returned while she put her arm around Ashley's waist.

Our time was about up, and Hannah had hardly spoken to Ashley. I was doing my best to keep it together and put on a cheerful face, but on the inside, I wasn't feeling cheery at all. Hannah had just received a death sentence, and here we were, pretending to be friends with someone we'd never see again. It all felt false. I thought maybe Hannah just didn't feel well. Maybe she was embarrassed about her thinning hair and casual dress. Maybe at her age, it wasn't only what was on the inside that counted.

We left the agency and walked back across the street to our hotel room. Hannah lay down on the bed and promptly fell asleep.

That was it? Her big wish, meeting her idol, and it's over?

Hannah looked up to Ashley and probably in her wildest dreams had thought she, too, could become a professional singer or dancer. Now, with her new diagnosis, how much of a future did she have? I still didn't want to accept her fate. And now that our fabulous wish trip was over, I felt nothing but sadness.

A night out at the movies with the girls

Room service!

Lounging by the pool

Meeting Ashley Tisdale

11

The Unhappiest Place on Earth

Meeting Ashley wasn't the only wish Hannah was granted in the summer of 2009. When the Make-A-Wish Foundation couldn't accommodate her pop-star dream, Hannah chose a Disney Cruise as an alternative. And since her team at Children's wanted us to hurry up with taking a big trip, the cruise was expedited. This rush meant sailing in the Bahamas during the hottest, muggiest time of year.

I was hopeful about this chance for our family to get away and have some fun. I'd personally never wanted to go on a cruise. My parents had gone on a Caribbean cruise for their twenty-fifth wedding anniversary and reported that they'd had a great time. But a crowded boat, buffet tables piled with food, and potential seasickness never appealed to me.

When we boarded the plane at SeaTac and Hannah was invited to sit up front in the cockpit before takeoff, I started to think this trip might not be so bad after all. We were seated in coach on the way to Florida, but we were given first-class treatment, thanks to Make-A-Wish.

Once we had boarded the Disney ship and were shown to our staterooms, I thought, *Wow, this is going to be fun!* Ryan and Andrew initially loved having their own quarters, ordering room service any time of the day, and enjoying the freedom to come and go as they pleased on the ship. I enjoyed dressing up and going to dinner as a family. Hannah initially seemed thrilled with the ship and the Disney gifts that she'd received from the foundation. But pretty soon the shine wore off, she began to grumble, and I started feeling like we were in the unhappiest place on Earth.

I couldn't comprehend or accept the knowledge that my daughter was going to die sometime soon. As I walked around the ship, checking out the pools, the game rooms, the theaters, all I could think about was how much fun my formerly active, independent, and social girl would have had on this cruise before she had cancer. Now I only saw what Hannah couldn't do.

She had chosen a Disney Cruise largely based on the Disney Channel shows she watched at home. Most of the shows were musical, like *Hannah Montana*, but she was also a regular for *The Suite Life of Zach and Cody* and *Wizards of Waverly Place*. Those characters weren't part of this cruise, and since Hannah wouldn't join in with the teen activities on board, she rolled her eyes and complained, "This is too Mickey Mouse for me."

More and more, she leeched onto us and shrank from the oppressive heat, mostly wanting to stay onboard instead of taking excursions on land. Even our trip to meet the dolphins in Nassau turned into an endurance test as we sweated in our wetsuits through the multiple lines just to get in the water. The only good time our family had was playing bingo on the air-conditioned ship.

Eventually the boys got sick of each other, and I got sick of it being the two of them and the three of us. In their close quarters on the last night before the ship docked back in Florida, Ryan and Andrew fought—literally throwing fists at each other until they had to be separated. I lay awake for the rest of the night with Ryan now bunked in our room. I couldn't wait to get off the ship.

Just when I thought it couldn't get worse, it did. We had checked into an airport hotel for the day since we had a long layover before our flight home. Then violent thunderstorms threatened to cancel our flight. When Bill couldn't get any information from the airline, he left our room to go check on the plane's status. On cue, Andrew became sick with a fever and vomiting. Here I was left alone with a sick kid, an angry kid, and a kid who could do very little for herself.

When Bill called for us to meet him at the airline gate because the flight was ready to depart, I was furious that I had to manage the luggage, all of our stuff, and our three kids—two of whom couldn't help at all—by myself. In desperation, I gave Andrew some of Hannah's medications and shuttled everyone out of the hotel room. I was bound and determined to not get stuck in Florida one more day. I wanted nothing more at this point than to go home. This seemed a fitting ending to the family vacation I had not hoped for.

After the trip to meet Ashley fizzled out, this was just one more disappointment. If Hannah's condition was only going to get worse, I wondered if and when we would be able to take another vacation. So much joy and fun had been taken from our family since her diagnosis. I wasn't sure how we could sustain ourselves. And I was wishing more and more for the daughter I used to know.

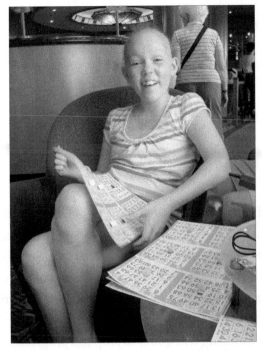

Bingo!

Meeting a dolphin in Nassau

12

Gamma Knife

In the fall of 2009, I still didn't want to believe that Hannah's cancer had returned and that she would die. She still wasn't symptomatic, so I began to question the doctors. They patiently listened to me as I suggested new drugs and therapies I had come up with from my online searches. They even supported the holistic methods that Hannah had incorporated to save herself. But they kept coming back to the same endgame: nothing was going to stop the progression of Hannah's cancer.

Spurred on by what I was reading and hoping to discover, I attended a conference in Ashland, Oregon, focused on alternative treatments for brain cancer. One of the presenters was Dr. Jim Olson. When Hannah relapsed in the spring, Bill and I had turned to Dr. Olson not only as a member of her treatment team at Children's but also as a specialist in her type of tumor and the head of her research study. He could only hug us and say, "I'm so sorry."

But here was Dr. Olson at the conference, giving a presentation about ongoing studies in his lab. I was riveted. I met another mom that weekend who, like me, was looking for hope. Margo had an older son who had relapsed multiple times with the same brain tumor as Hannah's. A Stanford grad, she was smart and quick and cautioned me to not accept what I was hearing from our doctors. Margo questioned everything—the scans, the therapies, and the terminal prognosis. She gave me added fuel to fight the new diagnosis, especially since Hannah had yet to show any clinical signs of illness.

I returned to Seattle with gloves on, ready to fight for my daughter. That fight came to an abrupt halt after the next MRI scan. The test indicated that the tumor was progressing. I saw the film with my own eyes. Even though Hannah didn't appear sicker, the cancer was growing. As Dr. Geyer talked to us about different therapies to try, I started to realize that this wasn't about trying to cure Hannah, but rather about buying her more time.

After we discussed the options with Dr. Geyer, the most logical step was to give her a type of radiation that she hadn't had yet: Gamma Knife surgery. It made perfect sense to me to try this targeted therapy that would literally and precisely blast the cancer cells in her brain. It was a onetime procedure on an outpatient basis, unlike the six weeks of radiation she had already endured. I could get on board, and so could Bill, because it was something new to try. Hannah didn't argue the choice but said she was mad that her visualizations and belief that she was killing and shrinking the tumors didn't work.

The Gamma Knife procedure was scheduled for mid-November at Harborview Medical Center, the only place connected to Children's Hospital that had the equipment. We were also hoping that the date we scheduled for the procedure would give Hannah enough time to recover and to attend Adam and Alexis's wedding at the end of December.

I had worked at Harborview as a psychiatric occupational therapist before I had children. It was strange to go back to the place I had worked for a very different reason.

Walking down the long basement corridors to the treatment room, I had a terrible feeling. Bill and Hannah seemed calm, but I wasn't. I thought I had been through enough to be prepared, but I was wrong. I found this therapy to be the most barbaric yet. After Hannah was under general anesthesia, Bill and I waited in a nearby room as the surgeon put screws in her skull to secure her head to a precise spot on the table. It was hard to picture, and for a brief time, I thought I would faint.

After she was ready, we watched through an observation window as the doctors used tools that looked like they belonged in an auto shop to adjust the table and equipment. The treatment took hours and did nothing to relieve my worry. The final insult, to me, was when one of the senior physicians shook his head, looked at Hannah in recovery, and said, "It always happens to the pretty ones."

Hannah woke up from the procedure groggy but fairly unfazed. She had two large bandages on her forehead where the screws had been inserted. We pushed her in the wheelchair back down the long hallways to the parking garage. I felt no better than I had that morning, walking in the opposite direction. I wasn't sure we'd made the right decision.

We still had great hopes that the Gamma Knife radiosurgery would be successful. At first it appeared that it had been; Dr. Geyer showed us the dissolving tumors on the scan pictures. Hannah recovered physically from the procedure, but in the end, it took its toll on her mentally. She was robbed of more of her cognition—her memory, her focus, her problem solving. Hannah had prided herself on her intelligence. Now, in hopes of saving her life, we had given permission to strip more of that from her. I no longer held the delusion that Hannah's cancer hadn't returned. It seemed we were losing her one piece at a time.

13

Adam and Alexis's Wedding

It was freezing cold, even for New York at the end of December. The frigid air made me catch my breath as we stepped out of the taxi. Our family and Claude's had arrived for the wedding that was to take place on New Year's Eve in the city. Adam and Alexis had originally planned to get married in the summer, but with the uncertainty of Hannah's future, they decided to move it up six months. This trip was so different from our vacation the year before. Living under the black cloud of Hannah's relapse, it probably felt colder than it really was.

We checked into a Hilton hotel right across from Ground Zero. The place was fancy and all decked out for the holidays. The festive atmosphere almost made me forget that Hannah was sick. But then, all I had to do was look over to where the twin towers had stood to remember. Hannah had recovered fairly well from the Gamma Knife procedure. The girl loved a wedding, so adrenaline probably gave her more energy for the planned celebrations.

Before the rehearsal dinner, we toured the city wrapped in scarves, hats, and mittens. Andrew chose to skip the excursion. I hated that he was staying back at the hotel by himself, but I could only worry about one child at a time. Hannah insisted on ice skating in Central Park. It took Linda and me on either side of her to keep her upright. She fell a few times but got right back up and tried again. Hannah was a much stronger skater before she was diagnosed with cancer, but her spirit hadn't waned.

On the way back to the hotel for the dinner, we stopped at the Plaza Hotel. Hannah and the boys had grown up watching the *Home Alone* movies, so we had to check out the lobby. Hannah and I stood in front of a massive Christmas tree while Bill took our picture. We took more pictures that evening in the Hilton lobby, when we were all dressed up.

Recording these moments started me thinking of all that Hannah would miss in the future. She wouldn't live to return and stay in the Plaza. She would never see another brother get married. She would never have her own wedding.

The wedding was a black-tie affair held in a mansion on the Upper East Side. Hannah wore a short silver-and-black junior bridesmaid dress with black patent leather shoes. She looked stunning, even with her cropped hair. During the photo shoot before the wedding, Adam and Alexis made sure to arrange pictures taken with just them and Hannah.

As the ceremony began, Hannah was the first one to walk down the aisle. I detected some soft murmurings when the guests caught a glimpse of her barely-there hair and shaky gait. The family knew what she'd been through, but obviously not every guest did. Still, I was proud of her. I tried to silence the negative thoughts in my head about this wedding being Hannah's last. For the most part, I succeeded.

After dining and dancing and toasting the night away, Hannah was done. She asked me to sit with her in one of the living rooms and wait out the clock striking midnight. Riding home on the party bus back to the hotel, Hannah leaned her head on my shoulder and fell asleep.

Shortly after we arrived home, we learned that another couple's story was ending. Claude announced that he was leaving Linda and moving to New York. We were all shocked. My immediate reaction was to tell my brother that I loved him and would support him no matter what. My automatic response to any crisis involving Claude had always been unconditional love. The rest of my family and friends were not only surprised at his announcement, but also upset that Claude was leaving me at a time when I was losing Hannah. With my daughter in such a fragile state, I had no room in my head or heart to contemplate this new loss.

Bundled up with Ryan and cousins at Rockefeller Center

Hannah and I before the wedding

Adam and Alexis's wedding
(photo courtesy of Christian Oth Photography)

14

Hannah's Hopeful Hearts

Once we came home from the wedding, I moved into serious event planning. Still holding onto dim hope for Hannah's survival, I needed to put my focus on something purposeful. After the brain tumor conference in Oregon, I had cooked up an idea to hold a fundraiser to support Dr. Olson's lab. I'd had previous experience as an event planner, so the evening quickly formed in my mind.

Jim would present his research, two inspirational speakers would share their stories, and we would raise as much money as possible. Our home church, Grace Episcopal, would be the venue. I'd hire a caterer to provide a buffet. We wouldn't sell tickets or have a silent auction, but we would make a direct call for donations. Bill and I would cover the event costs so all of the money taken in would go to the Olson Lab. Most of all, we would do *something* to help kids with brain cancer. It may have been too late for Hannah, but I had found my cause.

We named our fundraising group Hannah's Hopeful Hearts. Our first event, in March 2010, was titled, "Climbing Mountains for a Cure for Brain Cancer." In addition to Dr. Olson sharing his lab's current work, I was thrilled to have these two speakers: Cheryl Broyles, a glioblastoma survivor, who told of surviving multiple cancer recurrences and of climbing Mount Shasta in celebration, and world-renowned alpine climber Ed Viesturs, who spoke about the teamwork necessary to tackle the largest mountains in the world under the most difficult conditions.

Hannah was present for this full-house event, proudly sitting with me up front, listening to the presentations and applauding wildly when donors' paddles raised over $100,000. The only time Hannah became emotional, put down her head, and cried, was when her friends sang Miley Cyrus's "The Climb." I was, of course, emotional the entire night and still clinging to some hope that Hannah would survive her own climb.

The event was such a success that for a while I believed that some of the money we had raised could save Hannah.

Cheryl's story was miraculous. Most adults with her cancer don't live for more than a year or two after diagnosis. But there she was, standing before us, telling us how many times she had beaten her brain tumor. Ed had faced multiple life-and-death situations in the most extreme Himalayan conditions and had lived to tell the tale. Jim introduced innovative ideas to conquer childhood cancer in ways that wouldn't harm the child the way traditional therapies did.

Before that night, I had no idea how poorly childhood cancer research is funded. With a very small percentage of federal dollars going to pediatrics, researchers such as Dr. Olson have to rely on private foundation grant money and community events to support their work. Families of the patients Jim has cared for put on most of those fundraising events, sometimes with and sometimes in memory of their children. Jim feels a personal calling to find safer cures for all cancers, especially for those that are currently inoperable or carry no survival rate. In a 2013 TED talk, Jim would say, "Maybe I was put on this earth to take care of these families, to walk the journeys with them that they didn't want to walk." We were proud to support Jim's work and grateful to have him on Hannah's team.

Hannah shone that night. Her hair had grown out somewhat, she looked beautiful in a new dress, and she wore a smile that wouldn't quit. Most of all, I was happy to see her surrounded by her girlfriends. For so long, Hannah had clung to Bill and me. Now she was in her element, talking and laughing with her friends. I kept being surprised when I didn't know where she was every minute of the evening. This was the old Hannah—confident, upbeat, and social. I knew this Hannah wouldn't last. But I loved having her back.

Hannah and friends at the
HHH fundraiser

With lifelong friend Lindsay, after the event

Bringing more hope and new life with
kitten, Milo, and friend Shania

15

Airlift

It was the Fourth of July—but not like the typical Fourths our family had spent on Bainbridge in years past. For us there would be no hometown parade, no street dance, no firework parties. We'd had a quiet day at home. That night, Bill barbecued burgers and corn on the grill. After dinner, Hannah and I sat together on a lounge chair on our back deck. The stars came out as we cuddled together under a blanket. Bill and the boys let off a few fireworks in the backyard over our pond. But soon the day fizzled out like an old sparkler, and we went to bed. I missed holiday gatherings and laughing with friends. Our world was becoming much smaller and quieter.

The next day dawned, but not so peacefully. I woke up to Hannah crying and calling out, "Mom, I need you."

I went to her room and found her curled up in a ball on her bed with her hands over her head. "Bad headache again?" I asked her.

She whimpered and nodded. By now I knew the drill. I retrieved the meds from the bathroom. We had some pretty powerful painkillers at the ready. She took the pills, and I continued to sit with her, rubbing her back, and waiting for the pain to pass. But her headache wouldn't go away. She writhed and cried, unable to get comfortable.

I left her room for a minute to get a glass of water. When I returned, Hannah was suddenly different. I asked, "How ya doing?" She couldn't speak or answer me. Her eyes were wide with alarm. Startled, I said, "Hannah, Hannah, are you okay?" No response. Even though she was awake, she seemed far away.

When I couldn't get her to answer any of my simple questions, I knew I needed help. Fortunately, I had spoken with Cory days earlier after Hannah's MRI showed significant disease progression. Cory had said, "If you encounter a problem and don't know what to do, call for help." So I yelled to Bill, who was downstairs, "Call 911!"

Within minutes I heard the siren of the ambulance getting louder as it approached our house. Medics rushed into Hannah's bedroom. With a shaking voice, I gave them details: "Hannah is eleven years old. She has brain cancer. She'd been having a terrible headache this morning, which we couldn't stop with the meds we had."

After a brief exam, one of the EMTs said, "We should call for an airlift. We need to get her to Children's as quickly as possible."

Once again, I was in disbelief. I asked the medics if it was necessary. And then I started to panic. Was this it? Were we losing our daughter right now?

I was allowed to ride to the fire station with Hannah in the back of the ambulance. She was restless but still couldn't speak. Bill followed us in his car. Shortly after we arrived, the helicopter landed in the field next to the station. I was shaking and could barely breathe for fear, but, mercifully, Hannah wasn't aware of what was happening. We know several firefighters on the island, but the only one I recognized at the station that day was a volunteer who happened to also be Andrew's chemistry teacher. I said to him, "This is Andrew's sister. Please take care of her."

There wasn't room in the helicopter for Bill and me to ride with Hannah, so we said goodbye to her on the stretcher, not knowing if we would see her alive again. We raced in our car to catch the next ferry, which was about to leave. At the ferry dock, we sped through the tollbooth without paying, not wanting to miss the boat. Ferry crew came running and screamed at us until we told them that our daughter was being airlifted. Hannah's flight from Bainbridge Island to Seattle Children's took just six minutes. Our ride to the hospital seemed to take forever.

By the time we arrived, Hannah had already been processed through the ER, given a CT scan, and admitted to the ICU. When we saw her, she was still nonverbal but awake and fairly agitated. It was hard to know how to comfort her. The doctors said the CT didn't show a bleed or anything more unusual, but they didn't know what was wrong with her. It was later determined that Hannah likely had suffered a massive seizure.

Family and friends arrived at the hospital off the next boat. Linda brought Ryan and Andrew with her, and my friends Nancy, Barb, Jen, and Sara, came as well. We sat around Hannah's bed, fearful and not knowing what would happen next. The boys looked at their sister and offered a few quiet words, but they didn't know what to say to her any more than the rest of us did.

Shortly after everyone had gathered, an attending oncologist came to speak with Bill and me. He gently suggested that since Hannah's condition was terminal, we could choose to decline any extraordinary life-sustaining treatment for her in the ICU. Bill and I hadn't even signed a DNR (do not resuscitate) form, but this was only the beginning of the impossible questions and decisions, less about therapies and more about Hannah's remaining days.

Later that same day, in a private room on the cancer ward, we continued to watch and wait. The boys had gone home with Linda, but my friends stayed with us. I said to Nancy, "I can't lose her. What if she never comes out of this?" Nancy only shook her head and murmured, "I'm so sorry." We were both crying.

After my friends left, Hannah started to speak again, but it was nonsense. Bill and I laid down on either side of Hannah's bed in separate cots. As I closed my eyes and started to replay the events of the day in my head, I suddenly heard a voice: "Hey, are you guys awake?"

It was our friend and priest, Bill, making a late-night hospital call. He whispered a prayer and said goodnight. Despite the calamities of the day, we knew our friends and family held us in love.

The next morning, our remarkable daughter woke up. She was as clear as day, talking with us like her normal self and asking questions about why she was in the hospital. She had no idea what had transpired in the previous twenty-four hours. She didn't remember the helicopter ride, the ICU, or any of the visitors. Hannah joked with the nurses and doctors about the wild day and night she'd been told she had.

Our prayers had been answered. We'd gotten our daughter back. But where would we go from there? How much more time did we have with Hannah? Every day now felt precious.

Grumpy Hannah

Relaxing with Dad on the beach

Bill with our friend, priest, and Little
League co-coach, Bill, in happier
times

16

A Trip to the Beach

At Hannah's discharge from what I speculated would be her last inpatient stay, Bill and I opted for one more last-chance round of chemotherapy. We also agreed that it was time to bring hospice on board, as we needed more assistance at home.

That decision was one I had dreaded, as it seemed to set the countdown clock to the end. But given the nightmarish experience of the airlift, it didn't seem so terrible. Asking for additional help was just the next right step. Even more important than getting extra help was finding something to do as a family, knowing our time with Hannah was running out.

We quickly formulated a plan to go to the Oregon coast. Our family had spent several glorious vacations on that beach over the years. In the height of summer, we couldn't find a place to stay at Cannon Beach, where we'd always gone. But we did find a house to rent in Manzanita, just south of there.

At the start it felt like any other vacation. Hannah watched movies on her portable DVD player while the boys slept most of the way on the car ride down. When we arrived, we fell in love with the midcentury home, but the unfamiliar grassy beach felt a little strange, different from the wide-open sands of Cannon Beach. At least Ryan and Andrew were happy to have rooms in a separate garage annex attached to the home, while Hannah was delighted to have her bed in an alcove next to Bill's and my room.

On the first evening we ate pizza and played cards. As we sat on the floor around the coffee table, Hannah laughed and made jokes. It was hard to imagine that she'd been airlifted to the hospital only a few weeks earlier.

The next day, I'd scheduled a mini spa day for Hannah and myself, complete with massages and pedicures. Since she'd relapsed, Hannah had been getting weekly half-hour massages on Bainbridge. I believed her sessions with Lily were therapeutic, and after she'd been through so much pain and torture, Bill and I wanted to give her this small amount of comfort.

Before we left to go to the spa, I helped Hannah take a bath. She had been pretty weak since the seizure and needed more help to take care of herself—another reminder that she was losing her independence. I was surprised when she started talking to me as she sat in the tub. I'd been waiting and hoping for Hannah to talk about how she was feeling. I wondered if she knew she was dying. My daughter who usually shared everything with me had been either unable or unwilling to say how she felt.

"This is so hard," she suddenly cried out. As I helped her out of the bath, she collapsed in my arms, saying, "I feel like I've taken ten steps forward and a thousand steps back."

My first instinct was to comfort her and say something like, "You're so strong. You've been through so much, and you haven't given up." But then I realized she was doing just what I had hoped she would do: telling me how she felt. I wrapped a towel around her and pulled her onto my lap. "I know. I'm so sorry, Hannah. I love you so much."

The morning after our spa treatments, she woke up with another headache. With the help of hospice, we now had the big-gun pain relievers. But once again, the meds weren't helping. After the last scary trip to the hospital precipitated by an unrelenting headache, I worried that Hannah was going to have another massive seizure—far from home and medical support.

After sitting with Hannah on her bed for a while, Bill and I moved to the living room couch. We waited for the meds to kick in and listened to Hannah moan and cry. I couldn't stand it. I cried right along with her as Bill hugged me. Just when I thought I'd had enough, she yelled to us, "I love you so much!" It was heartbreaking. My daughter was dying, and it seemed she was trying to make us feel better.

When Hannah's headache wouldn't stop, I called Cory. "It's up to you," she said calmly. "We wouldn't do anything different from what you're giving her. But if you'd feel better, give her more medicine and drive home." That was all the permission I needed to hear. "We're going home," I announced. I needed to be closer to the hospice staff and any emergency services we might need.

The boys were furious. Ryan said, "So what was the point of this family vacation?" I didn't have an answer for him other than to say, "I'm sorry. We need to get home." It's so hard to meet everyone's expectations on a family trip, especially when traveling with someone who is very sick and needing constant care. I remember thinking that Ryan and Andrew had been dealt a shitty hand.

The boys had been through their own trauma on the sidelines of Hannah's illness. Often separated from me when I was with Hannah at the hospital, they were forced as young teens to become more grown up, more self-reliant. Quiet, gentle Andrew never complained or said a word about how Hannah's illness inconvenienced him or the family. But still, it took its toll on him. Ryan was the more vocal of the two, often ready to speak up for what he thought was right or when he thought he'd been wronged. Our family had been turned upside down, with Hannah's needs taking priority over the boys'. Gone were fun, light family vacations, as most of our energy necessarily revolved around Hannah.

Mercifully, my daughter slept on the five-hour drive home from Oregon. When we arrived, we carried her to her room and put her to bed. And she slept. The next day, as she slept on, I started to worry that she wouldn't wake up. I feared that we'd given her too much pain medication. An on-call hospice nurse came to examine her and echoed my concerns. She believed that Hannah was actively dying. This terrifying roller coaster ride wouldn't stop. "Is this it?" I wondered out loud. My girl continued to sleep through the day.

I spent a sleepless, tearful night in her bed, listening to her breathe. The next morning, another hospice nurse came to see Hannah, who was mostly unresponsive, had quit peeing, and was now breathing irregularly. The nurse and on-call doctor concurred with what the nurse had seen the day before. Hannah was dying.

We called Adam and Alexis. Bill phoned friends and family, who began showing up as I stayed in bed with Hannah. Soon there were enough people in our house that it began to feel like some surreal party. Before I knew it, there was a barbecue going and quite a gathering of people in our house and on the back deck. Through Hannah's open window, I heard laughter intermingled with softly spoken words. I kept wishing there was a different reason for the party.

I was extremely grateful for the folks who showed up, bringing flowers, food, and so much love. I couldn't leave Hannah's side, so one by one, people quietly visited us in her room. Night came, and everyone left. Bill went to sleep in our bed. I tried to stay awake for Adam and Alexis's arrival, but I didn't hear them when they came in after midnight. We all went to sleep wondering if Hannah would survive the night.

At 3:00 a.m. I awoke to Hannah's voice. "Mom?" She was awake. Once again, seemingly miraculously, she had recovered. Friends and family returned to our house. Linda came bright and early when she heard the news. Adam and Alexis not only kept Hannah company and made her laugh but gave me a break. Alli, who thought she had said goodbye to Hannah the day before, came back with her parents to see her miracle little sister. Alli then announced that she had canceled her trip to Europe in order to be near Hannah in the coming days.

For the rest of the weekend, Jeanette kept putting out meals from the kitchen. Bill's business partner, Mark, and his wife, Maureen, brought more food, including freshly caught salmon. By the end of Sunday Maureen, who had also tutored Hannah, became known as the "beer and pastries Sherpa." Hannah was able to join us downstairs, and the gathering became a fun celebration unlike the dismal evening the night before.

As much as I loved these people, their care and attention started to become overwhelming. I wanted time alone with our immediate family, especially my daughter. I was numb and exhausted from the events of the past week. I felt relieved that Hannah was no longer in pain and that we hadn't lost her. But the reality of Hannah's repeated retreats from death's door was taking its toll on me.

I wasn't ready for her to die. I wanted more time. I wanted to talk with her more. I wanted to hear her final wishes. I wanted another reprieve. I wanted a miracle. I wondered how long Hannah's body could keep fighting. I definitely wasn't sure how much more my heart could take.

Waking up with Alli and Dad

Everyone gathered around Hannah, the morning after

17

Hannah's Birthday

The day before Hannah's twelfth birthday, she began hallucinating. She reported hearing and seeing people around her that weren't evident to me.

"That lady has red lipstick on," she said, pointing to someone she saw sitting next to her. And later, laughing out loud when she was listening to some man we couldn't hear, she commented, "He's really funny." Hannah didn't seem disturbed by these visions.

I was curious. "Do you know who that is?" I asked her. I wondered if she was having visits from relatives who had passed before her. Still struggling to connect with Hannah about her feelings around death, I hoped that she would tell me more about her experiences with spirits.

On Hannah's birthday the hallucinations became more of a frightened delirium. Hannah began to squirm and jump from her spot on the couch. "There's bugs crawling all over me!" she yelled. The visitors the day before had fascinated her, but now she was startled. She said there were people and cats popping up all around her. Not wanting to see her in more distress, I said yes to the doctor's offer of an antipsychotic medication. It took the rest of the day for Hannah to calm down.

Few people knew that she was having this new trouble. Alli and two other friends brought birthday balloons and gifts, but Hannah couldn't really focus on them. I watched their visits from across the room, waiting for the new meds to kick in. Hannah seemed to be paying more attention to her internal stimuli than to her visitors. I also suspected that Hannah couldn't see very well anymore. She kept her eyes closed as the two friends tried to show her a photo scrapbook they'd made of their times together.

Days earlier, when Hannah and I were lying in her bed, I had put the *Mamma Mia!* DVD in her portable player. Hannah kept turning the movie off and on, and finally she slammed the player shut in frustration. It suddenly dawned on me that she couldn't see the screen.

The evening of her birthday, Linda and the cousins came over for dinner and cake. Hannah sat by herself on the couch, not joining us at the table. When I carried the cake out to her in the living room while everyone sang "Happy Birthday," Hannah tried blowing the candles out in the wrong direction. Apparently she couldn't see the cake. Hannah used to love birthdays, but there wasn't much to love about her twelfth.

As the next few days passed, Hannah was more at peace. She didn't seem to be having scary hallucinations anymore, but she was still having visions. One day she looked toward the French doors of our den and said, "That girl looks like Courtney, but I don't know her." I didn't see anyone through the doors. A couple nights later, when I was putting Hannah to bed, she saw the girl again and said, "I don't know if I can be friends with someone I don't know."

The first time it happened, I called my friend Karen. She had lost her twelve-year-old daughter, Katie, to cancer just months before Hannah was diagnosed. Karen told me that she had been out walking and talking to Katie at the same time Hannah was seeing the strange girl. Karen had told Katie, "Be ready to meet Hannah." The synchronicity gave me chills. Karen and I believed that Katie would be there to greet Hannah when she passed.

I was fascinated by the accounts of dying people who could see loved ones who had passed on before them right before their death. On our aborted trip to Oregon, I was reading the book *Final Gifts,* by Maggie Callanan and Patricia Kelley. The authors explained a phenomenon common among people who are dying:

The most prevalent theme in Nearing Death Awareness seems to be the presence of someone not alive. The timing varies; the experience can happen hours or days or sometimes weeks before the actual death. Dying people often interact with someone invisible to others—talking to them, smiling or nodding at them. Sometimes, more than one invisible person is involved. The unseen person's identity often is clear to the dying. Generally they recognize someone significant from their lives—parent, spouse, sibling, friend—who is already dead. There is often a sense of pleasure, even of joyful reunion, in seeing that person again. Some see religious figures—angels, perhaps, or spirits. Even when people don't recognize the figure they're seeing they don't appear upset or frightened. Most accept these other presences without question.

I wondered who would be there to meet Hannah when she passed. Besides the loss of a couple of beloved pets, Hannah had limited experience with death. She only knew Bill's mom, who had died the summer before she got sick. Of course, plenty of other family members had passed before, but I fretted that Hannah didn't know them in this life and therefore wouldn't recognize anyone in the hereafter. Still, even though she didn't know Katie, Hannah seemed more curious to meet her than frightened by the vision. I was comforted to know that another young girl who had died too soon would be there when Hannah transitioned to another state of being.

Hannah not seeing her birthday cake

Jade and Courtney sharing their photo album with
Hannah

18

Will There Be Cake?

The house was growing quiet. Hannah slept for longer and longer periods of time. She was eating and drinking less. Each week, I worried more and more that she wouldn't wake up. I dreaded Thursdays; that was the day her pain would spike and we had to increase the meds, after which she slept for days. At least she seemed comfortable. But all I wanted was for her to wake up. Each time she did, Cory would say to me, as I'd heard her say before whenever Hannah demonstrated some superhuman feat, "Have you met your daughter?"

As much as I wanted Hannah to be awake, home was not so peaceful when she was. She was often extremely moody. The doctors attributed her emotional state to the growing cancer and the steroids. Her outbursts were nearly unbearable. It was hard enough to be losing my daughter, but in the little time we had she was also not her old sweet self. Hannah would yell and say hurtful things to me. She would order me to fetch her things and then insult me in the process. I learned to walk away from her, knowing that with her poor short-term memory, she would forget a few minutes later what she had asked me for or why she was so upset. This survival tactic seemed mean, but it was necessary for my sanity. I hated every minute of those interactions.

On my birthday, August 10, I'd had enough. I walked away from a ranting Hannah, sat outside on the back deck, put my head in my hands, and started to cry. *Please, God. Have mercy on Hannah. I can't take this anymore! I know she's dying, but she's miserable. We're all miserable. Please end this.*

Not knowing what else to do, I talked to Dr. Geyer on the phone about her extreme mood swings. He said, "Well, we can lower the steroid dose, but then we'd likely have to increase the pain medication as her headaches return." I knew the steroids were decreasing the inflammation in her brain as the cancer grew, but it seemed crueler to keep Hannah in this state. After talking it over with Bill, I said, "Okay, let's do it." Based on my mom's experience with painkillers at the end of her life, I knew I had just precipitated my daughter's death.

At the same time, as I was growing less able to handle Hannah's care, and knowing that her death was days or weeks away, the hospice team gently proposed that they could give her palliative sedation. This would put Hannah into a coma state, presumably until she passed. Frankly, I was shocked that we were being offered a choice usually reserved for pet owners. But I was also exhausted from watching Hannah vacillate between coma-like sleep and ranting anger. Bill and I didn't know what to do. We thought about the options for a few hours until Hannah woke up again, giving us our answer. She wasn't done yet.

By mid-August Hannah was often only semiconscious, barely able to stay awake with the increased dose of narcotics. I felt grateful that she was finally calm and peaceful, but now I missed my daughter. I longed to have a meaningful conversation with her, even though I knew that was unlikely. I wanted her to talk about how she felt and tell me if she had any final wishes.

Completely out of the blue one day, she asked the question, "Will there be cake?"

"For what?" I asked.

"For my celebration," she said.

"For your birthday?" I asked, thinking she was confusing her birthday for mine, which had happened the week before.

"No, at Grace," Hannah said.

I was stunned. Was Hannah finally giving voice to the fact that she knew she was going to die? How long had she known? Was she already thinking about the memorial that would follow her death? Was she actually planning what she wanted at her service, just as she had planned and orchestrated hundreds of playdates with her friends? Was the food the most important piece, or was it just the easiest thing for her to speak about? Was this her one final wish?

For months after Hannah relapsed, we'd skirted around the subject of her death. When the scans showed that the cancer had returned, she had asked us right away, "Am I going to die?" The doctors had cautioned us to not answer the question directly, explaining that no one really knows when they're going to die. Maybe Hannah would be the rare exception. When she relapsed, I was not at all ready to accept that I would lose my daughter. It was impossible and inconceivable that she would die.

Now we were running out of time to have an honest conversation with her. We'd been torturing ourselves about when to speak with Hannah about the fact that she was going to die. Walking those fine lines between caring for our daughter, wanting to protect her, and not being able to stand the thought of losing her, we had kept the truth from her. And now here was Hannah, finally opening the door to let us know she was aware that she was dying.

There were other subtle hints that she knew death was coming. After weeks of not wanting her friends to visit, Hannah began allowing them to stop by the house. During the visits, some of the friends chatted away as if nothing was wrong, some cried silently at her side, and others simply couldn't show up, telling me they wanted to remember Hannah as they used to know her. She finally allowed friends to look at her unopened birthday cards and presents. Hannah was not able to speak much anymore, but some part of her must have known that her friends needed to say goodbye.

The year before she had asked hard and honest questions about death and dying. She had asked for the truth, and to this day we feel guilty that we didn't give it to her. We regret that we didn't give her the opportunity to explore what it would mean to die when she still could, before she was too cognitively compromised. Questions swirled in my head:

What did she think it would feel like? Was she scared? Did she believe her soul would live on? Did she think she would see us again? What did she want us to do with her body? How did she want to say goodbye? Was there anything important left for her to do before she died? We didn't have the answer to any of those questions. However, we did know that when we celebrated her life, there would be cake.

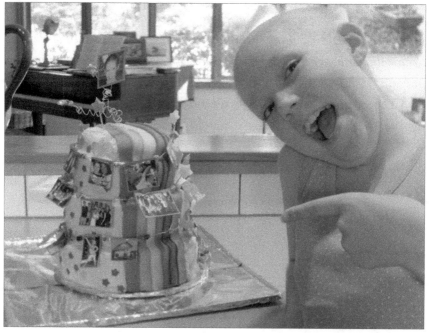

Hannah's special "Ace of Cakes" cake on her eleventh birthday

19

Saying Goodbye

Hannah was dying. For weeks I lay next to her in her bed, waiting for the inevitable. I was afraid to miss her leaving, so I seldom left her. I fumbled for words to say goodbye. I whispered to her, with tears rolling down my cheeks, "I know you have to go soon. I'll miss you, and I'll be very sad, but I'll be okay. You've made me a stronger person. I love you so much. I'm so glad that you were born and that you came to me." It was all true—except for the part about me being okay.

I hung on Hannah's every breath, wondering if it would be her last. I was exhausted from waking up in the middle of the night to check if she was still alive. During the day I watched her breathing, slow and steady. Her beautiful, graceful dancer's body was no longer muscular and strong, but too thin and bony. It was also strangely warm. I kept feeling her hands, her feet, her head, wondering when they would feel cold. She barely flinched at my touch.

The only way I could hold her as completely as I wanted to was to sit behind her, propped up by pillows, while she lay between my legs and slept against my chest. I did so for hours until my legs were numb. Once when I tried to move out from behind her, she came out of her deep sleep, grunted, and shook her head no, not wanting me to let her go. I held her longer. At least Hannah finally seemed to be at peace, no longer grimacing with pain.

After several days and moments of thinking, *This is it,* one morning her breathing changed. It was wet and raspy and rapid. The hospice nurse, Mary, arrived at 8:00 a.m. She started giving Hannah drops of a liquid meant to clear her throat. Bill and I took over, giving her more and more drops, suddenly scared and wondering if our daughter was dying at this very moment. Mary said, "It won't be long. Probably today." We called Adam and told him to catch the next flight he could.

I laid down next to Hannah with my arm supporting her neck and shoulders, and Bill laid down on her other side. I felt a strange mixture of fear, excitement, and anticipation, just as I had when I was about to give birth. Hannah actually looked as if she were in labor. There was a rhythm to her breathing. Her breaths would come hard and fast, followed by a rest period. I wondered if Hannah's body, at the end of its life, had to give birth to her soul.

I still wasn't ready to say goodbye, even though I kept telling her, "It's okay to go." Ryan and Andrew came and went from her bedroom, mumbling a few words here and there. Linda showed up to check on us. When she saw that Hannah was restless and struggling to breathe, she kissed her cheek, told her she loved her, and then sat on the floor at the foot of the bed, put her head down, and quietly prayed.

The boys came into the room and left again. I thought, *I wonder if they're tired of keeping up this vigil. Maybe they don't want to be present when their sister takes her last breath.* Bill left the bedroom for a few minutes to get coffee. I hadn't moved from my spot next to Hannah in nearly seven hours. As soon as Bill came back into the room, her breathing changed. It was slowing down, getting quieter, less effortful. I started silently counting the seconds between her breaths. As her breathing slowed, I told Bill, "I think she's going." And then it stopped.

I looked at my watch: 3:37 p.m. The astrologer in me needed to know the time of her death, which seemed just as important as knowing the time of her birth. I let out a sob. "Oh, Hannah." She was so still. I laid my hand on her chest. It didn't seem real that it wasn't moving. Where was she? Bill later told me that he immediately felt Hannah's spirit leave her body and rise up when she died, but I didn't feel that. I let out long, guttural sobs as I hugged her still body. I couldn't leave her. I had spent days telling her it was okay to go, but I knew it wasn't.

On this warm summer day, with the sun starting to go down behind the trees next door, I watched three drops of water slowly trickle down the window. I saw them as her tears at having to leave her family.

I lay with her for hours, my left arm still wrapped around her. People came and went. Ryan and Andrew said their goodbyes. Hospice staff came to make the official pronouncement of her death. Bill, our friend and priest, said a prayer. I couldn't stop crying.

When I finally unwrapped myself from Hannah and stood up, I felt dizzy and weak. I hadn't had anything to eat or drink since the night before. Just when I was about to go downstairs, Caroline walked into the bedroom. She sat down next to her cousin and started talking to her. I left the room to allow her some time with Hannah. Just as I was leaving, I ran into Ryan. With tears in his eyes, he hugged me, let out a big sigh, and with almost too much excitement said, "Now my life can finally begin." I felt as if my life was over.

That evening, I was alone with Hannah. The boys were together downstairs. Bill had gone to the airport to pick up Adam. Bill wanted to be the one to tell him that his little sister had died.

I had finally stopped crying, but Hannah's death still didn't seem real. It was so quiet in the house. I lit candles in Hannah's room, poured myself a glass of wine, and talked to her. I really didn't think she was still in her body, so I talked to her spirit, which I hoped was still lingering.

Eventually I got up the courage to bathe her body. I used a warm washcloth with water but no soap. After I dried her off, I spread rose lotion all over her skin, the same lotion we'd been using to massage her feet, her hands, and her back. And then I struggled to put her in the outfit I had picked out for her: the simple sleeveless white dress that she had worn to Adam's rehearsal dinner.

By the time Bill and Adam arrived home, I was finished with the bathing and dressing and talking. Adam sat on the bed and cried, talking to Hannah and saying his goodbyes. Shortly thereafter, a man and his sons from the local funeral home arrived. They were kind and caring. The sons were the same age as Ryan and Andrew. I figured they were used to the work, but I wondered how they felt about preparing a twelve-year-old's body.

They carried her out of her room, wrapped in her bedsheet, and Bill followed Hannah out of the house one last time. I sat on the stairs with Adam and sobbed as he put his arms around me.

I was definitely not okay.

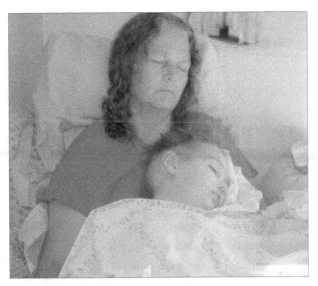

Supporting my sleeping daughter

Sleeping with Milo

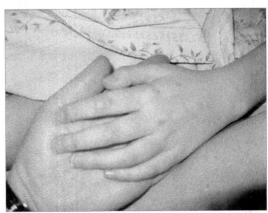

Hannah's hand in mine

20

The Early Days

Sleep came to me quickly the night Hannah died. I was exhausted from weeks of keeping watch over her. Now I could let go. I didn't have to worry or watch or wait for her death. It was over. I fell asleep, spent from crying, and hoped that she would visit me in my dreams.

I didn't dream of Hannah that first night. The next morning, I woke up and for a few blissful seconds forgot that she had died. This repeated every morning for weeks, and it was agony. I didn't want to get out of bed and face the truth of her passing. I lay in bed and replayed her final days, her final hours, like a gut-wrenching movie. These memories were accompanied by uncomfortable feelings—numbing fatigue, headaches, and even chest pain. I was surprised that my heart actually hurt from the grief. Part of me hoped that my heart would just stop so I could join Hannah.

Numb and sad, and despite my physical pains, I walked endless miles in the forest near our house. I didn't know what else to do in the days following her death. Surrounded by towering fir and cedar trees, I kept looking for Hannah in the shadows. I imagined her standing just behind the trees, watching me. I wished my brain would conjure up an image of her, but it never did. I had to be content with the belief that she was walking with me. The days were a blur, and I had no clear vision of where I was headed.

On these walks I began to contemplate an idea that I'd had when Hannah lay dying. I had started to see her as a separate entity from me. Of course, I knew she was her own person, but I was realizing that

Hannah was more than my daughter. She was a soul with a life purpose, and that purpose had been fulfilled. The girl whose body had been ravaged and poisoned by cancer and its treatment was more than her body. Hannah was a beautiful, brave, and impenetrable soul that had committed to a short life to love and be loved by her family and friends through the most terrible circumstances. I may have been protecting myself as I was preparing to lose her and wondering how I would survive, but in the days before her death, I had started looking at Hannah as an infinite soul.

Shortly before she died, I drew on astrology to help me find the meaning of Hannah's too-brief time on Earth. I'd been studying astrology for almost ten years and had a deep passion for the practice. I believe souls are on an evolving journey from one lifetime to the next. A soul's current incarnation is revealed in the birth chart, a map of sorts that serves as a blueprint or a lesson plan for a person's soul.

Questions tossed in my head: *What did Hannah's soul hope to achieve in this lifetime? Were there signs in her chart that she had reached the end of this incarnation? Why did she need to suffer and die in such a horrendous way? And what does my own chart say about why I gave birth to this daughter, to have her with me for just twelve short years?*

To find some of these answers, I turned to my astrology mentor and teacher, Steven Forrest. Days before Hannah died, I'd begun emailing Steve with questions while she lay sleeping next to me. He was very responsive. Years later, Bill and I would journey to Steve's home to have him read Hannah's chart, hoping to clarify my questions about why she'd been born and how my soul intertwined with hers.

My conversation with Steve began with questions about Mother Teresa. Call it serendipity or something else, but as Hannah lay dying, I learned that August 26 would have been Mother Teresa's one hundredth birthday. I started to wonder if Mother Teresa, or some archetype like her, had come into this lifetime in the form of Hannah.

I was probably searching for some balm to soothe my soul, comparing this saintly woman to my daughter. But looking at their astrological charts, I couldn't help but see a connection. From Steve I had learned to look at individuals compassionately. He also talked a lot about how karma worked with souls returning to repeat or heal past wounds. So, in my sleep-deprived head, I began to fantasize that Mother Teresa had reincarnated as Hannah. The dates matched up. Mother Teresa died in the fall of 1997, shortly before Hannah was conceived.

Following the way Steve told soul stories, I started to think about Mother Teresa, the woman who cared for the sick, dying, and unwanted, as choosing to experience a lifetime, like Hannah's, in which she was beloved but also experienced the other end of the spectrum, where people loved and cared for her until her death. Here was Hannah, experiencing an awful terminal illness, surrounded by the kind of support that Mother Teresa might have given Hannah, had she been born at a different time and place.

In our email exchange, Steve wrote, "The parallels between Mother Teresa and Hannah are eerie, both astrologically and also, in a deep way, biographically. I guess it is possible that Hannah is the literal reincarnation of Mother Teresa—come back to complete the 'study' by taking the suffering into her own body this time. At a broader level—well, who are we really? At one level of focus, we are individuals. At the other extreme, we are all One and the little self is an illusion. Somewhere in between we are individual expressions of universal archetypes."

Talking with Steve gave me some consolation that there had been a purpose to Hannah's short life, even if it meant she had finished what she came to do. I firmly believed that Hannah's life had meaning. I could rest somewhat in that knowledge, but I was still left with the utter sadness of her being gone. How was I going to continue living my life without her? If her soul was eternal, where did she exist? How could I find her or make contact with her? I had asked her on her deathbed to send me signs that she was okay. How long would I have to wait for her to send me a sign?

I was restless with the need to find Hannah. Despite what my head was telling me, and despite the relief that her suffering was over, my heart was aching.

21

A Resurrection Story

As Hannah had slept through the last days of her life here, I laid next to her and held her hand. I loved Hannah's hands, even though they reminded me of my mom's hands. She'd told me she hated the short thumbs that her grandmother had passed down to her. I read them as a sign that Mom had gifted Hannah to me.

These hands, which had been so busy and so adorned with little-girl nail polish, had rested still and unusually hot at her side. I had stared at the silver claddagh ring on her third finger that I had given to her when she finished chemo treatment. This traditional Irish ring takes the shape of two hands holding a heart and symbolizes love, loyalty, and friendship. I'd cried imagining the day that I would take this ring off Hannah's finger and put it on my own.

I had held Hannah's hand and her heart for twelve years. Her hands connected me with her, as she was often the first one to reach out and draw me in close. Her hands let me know when she wanted to share some happiness, fear, or secret. Hannah would cup her hands around my ear and whisper something to me that only I could know. Her hands told me that she needed me, and mine in turn told me that I needed her.

I couldn't imagine not holding Hannah's hand when she was gone. Before she passed, I lay next to her and asked her over and over to give me a sign that she was okay after she died. I also needed to know that she would be with me, near me somehow, and holding me close.

As much as I longed for it, I wasn't expecting to get a sign from Hannah soon after she died. Hannah passed on a Monday. On Thursday of that same week, Bill came rushing into our house and said, "I just got a call from Isabel. She said she has news about Hannah!"

Isabel was one of his former colleagues at work, but I was only acquainted with her. I knew her as a smart, serious, fifty-something law student with a captivating Irish accent who had helped us out at our first Hannah's Hopeful Hearts fundraiser. At the event, she and Hannah had sold glassybaby votives together. Even though I didn't know Isabel well, of course I wanted to hear anything she had to tell me about my daughter.

I called Isabel right away. She shared, "Hannah came to me in the law library today where I was studying. She was wearing a pink Washington State University sweatshirt. I noticed a worried look on her face so I asked her what was wrong. I thought she might be missing one of you, so I asked her, 'Is it your mom, your dad, one of your brothers?' Hannah nodded and said it was her brother Andrew. She said she was concerned about him. She also wanted to know that he would take care of the dogs and cats."

Andrew had adopted a golden-mix puppy a year before with Hannah's help. She told Isabel she especially wanted to know that this dog, Moose, would be okay. We had hoped that Moose would bring a spark of life back to Andrew. Anyone close to our family knew that we were worried about him too. Our formerly athletic, social, smart kid had become depressed, withdrawn, and seriously overweight in the past years. We were all concerned about our gentle giant, especially in light of Hannah's passing.

Isabel continued, "Hannah wouldn't leave me alone until I called you and Bill. She stood beside the study bench with her arms folded across her chest, glaring at me. I couldn't leave the library to go to my class. I finally gathered up my books and mustered up my courage to call you. It was intimidating!" Isabel described feeling an overwhelming sense of joy and happiness, but she didn't know where those feelings were coming from. After spending over an hour with Isabel, Hannah said to Isabel, "Tell them not to be afraid. There's nothing to be afraid of."

When Isabel watched Hannah leave—"skipping away," as she recalled it—she felt the joy and happiness leave her and realized it was Hannah carrying those feelings.

Isabel hadn't known us or our beliefs about the afterlife very well. But she followed Hannah's insistent directions to contact us, and I was so grateful that she did. Through Isabel, a virtual stranger to me, Hannah had found a way to reach out and deliver a message that she was okay.

Later that day, still glowing with the story of Hannah's visit to Isabel, we gathered the boys to tell them what we had heard. Adam, Ryan, and Andrew listened in stunned silence but didn't say much. Finally, Andrew said, "So Isabel didn't dream seeing Hannah? This was for real? Then heaven must be real."

Before Hannah died, I don't know that I could have said heaven was real. I was born and raised in a conservative Presbyterian church. From early childhood Sunday school classes to an active high school church group, I grew up with many Christian stories, beliefs, and songs. But I can't honestly say that I knew heaven or an afterlife was real—that souls continue to live on—until after I lost my daughter. Now, I thought, maybe I would see her watching me from behind the trees on my walks. She wasn't just gone.

Hannah appearing to Isabel, a kind of resurrection, was the first sign of many that Hannah was still alive in spirit form. It was remarkable that Hannah had delivered on my request for a sign so soon after she had passed. And it wasn't just any sign, but a clear vision with a message. For the first time in a very long while I felt hopeful again. I didn't have Isabel's gift of seeing beyond the veil to the realm where Hannah now lived, but I believed every word of her story. I wished I'd been the one my daughter had visited, but for now, it was enough. It was real proof to me that Hannah's spirit was alive.

As a flower girl with Andrew as ring bearer at a friend's wedding, 2002

Hannah, wearing her pink sweatshirt, and Andrew with baby Moose

Andrew with Moose and Buddy, 2014

22

Two Memorials

Whoa. Hannah was alive in spirit. I was incredibly grateful that she'd found a way to communicate with us through Isabel. Hearing from Hannah alleviated some of the pain of her death. I still faced the daunting task of learning how to live without her in my daily life, but now I could explore ways to contact her in the spirit world. First, though, there was the business of saying goodbye to her earthly life.

Hannah's memorial service wasn't scheduled for another week, but our priest friend, Bill, came up with the idea to invite her friends to gather informally at Grace Church on the Friday after she died. The new school year had just begun, and we were painfully aware that her girlfriends had received the news of Hannah's death just hours before they had to report to seventh grade.

It was a somber and tearful gathering at Grace that Friday afternoon. Tons of girls and their moms showed up at the church carrying bouquets of sunflowers, which they laid on the altar. Some of the girls had seen Hannah recently. Others, like her lifelong friend Lindsay, hadn't seen her all summer, choosing to remember Hannah as vital and happy. It was especially tough to see the ones who hadn't visited.

While they struggled with their emotions, I found myself unusually strong. The girls cried and said very little; I was calm and composed. I listened to them, hugged them, and supported them, as if I were their mother. One of the moms said, "We're sorry. It shouldn't be you comforting us." But I was really okay. I couldn't have been there for them days earlier, but it seemed that Hannah's spirit was giving me the strength I needed to support these friends. Perhaps hearing from Isabel the day before helped. Hannah had always been a source of strength and optimism for her friends. In some ways, I felt as if I were standing in for her.

A week later we returned to Grace for Hannah's memorial. I wasn't so confident I could keep it together through the service as well as I had with the girlfriends. Claude had come in from New York, and Bill's brothers and their families came from California. I was still struggling to cope with my brother's separation from me and his family, but I couldn't deal with that sadness on that day.

I was grateful when our priest friend, Bill, gathered our extended family in a private room beforehand. We joined hands in a large circle. Some said a few words. Others said prayers. I stood there wondering how in the world I was going to get through the next several hours. After Bill gave us communion, it was time. This quiet gathering helped settle my nerves before going into the church.

When I walked into the sanctuary, I couldn't believe my eyes. The church was completely full, with folks standing along the walls and spilling out into the narthex. I could only look for a few seconds before I put my head down. I was afraid to make eye contact for fear that I would lose the composure I had just gained. Thankfully, we were seated in the front row, facing away from the standing-room-only crowd.

Late-afternoon sunshine streamed through the large picture windows at the front of the church. I focused on the gorgeous flower arrangements that my friend Jen had created. Warmly lit glassybaby votive candles sat on the altar, encircling the large chocolate layer cake that Hannah had requested. When folks started singing the first song, "Let It Be," I began to cry. I suddenly didn't want to be there, and it didn't seem real that all of these people were gathered to say goodbye to my daughter. In that same mix of emotions was pride in this outpouring of sympathy for Hannah and our family. But the number of people who showed up underscored the magnitude of the loss.

I have said goodbye to many family members in my life, starting at a fairly young age. I've attended lots of funerals—grandparents, parents, in-laws, aunts, and uncles. I was devastated at my dad's, given his sudden death from a heart attack, and relieved at my mom's after her long suffering illness. I was probably still in shock from Hannah's death and also relieved that her suffering was over. Still, it felt like a bad dream that I'd had to orchestrate my daughter's memorial. At least I didn't have to stare at a casket at the front of the church.

We hadn't asked Hannah before she died what she wanted us to do with her body. Even though burial was customary for the parents and grandparents in Bill's and my family, he and I have decided to be cremated. But we had never directly asked Hannah if she wanted to be buried or cremated, and that haunted us for a long time. The only thing she had said out loud was, "Get rid of all of it," pointing to things in her room. I got the sense from Hannah at the end of her life that she didn't care what we did with her body or her belongings, much less how we would memorialize her. We would learn weeks after the service that we had unknowingly honored Hannah's wish. Courtney came to visit and shared with us, "When Hannah and I were at your beach house, we agreed that when each of us died, we wanted to be cremated and have our ashes scattered out there in the Puget Sound."

At the memorial, I calmed down again after the first song, as people got up to share their words about Hannah. Linda and Alexis read pieces that Hannah had written, including an essay from her last year of school in which she imagined her future self as a medical student, wanting to find a cure for pediatric cancer. I heard sniffles behind me as those gathered felt Hannah's hopefulness and what wasn't to be. I was proud of my brave, beautiful daughter.

After the words and the eulogies, Hannah's cousin Chris, Linda and Claude's son, sang a hauntingly beautiful version of "Hallelujah." The whole congregation joined in the chorus. The spirit I felt in the room during that song was palpable, and my tears began to dry up.

Bill and I hadn't planned to say a word at the service, mostly because we didn't think we'd make it through without bursting into tears. But, spontaneously, Bill got up and thanked the community for all the support we'd received during Hannah's illness.

I wish I'd had the courage to say, "Hannah's alive!" I wanted to share the good news that she was alive in spirit, as Isabel had described. I'd only shared this story with a few close friends and family. But this venue felt too large for such an intimate account, and I knew I wouldn't keep it together.

A couple other people I encountered after the service were not handling the event so well. I found Claude sobbing in the private room where we had gathered beforehand. He didn't say a word, but he didn't have to. I guessed that he was grieving not just for Hannah, but for the family and the life he had left behind. My head registered his sadness, but I didn't have room in my heart that day to respond to him other than offer a hug. The other person who surprised me was Grant, who years earlier had babysat Hannah and her brothers. When I hugged him, this strong college football quarterback burst into tears. He cried and could barely get out the words "I'm so sorry."

With the light now faded in the church, pictures of Hannah played on a large-screen television while her favorite music played in the background. I felt more grounded and composed than I had been at the start of the service. It was easier than I'd thought to embrace the folks who came up to offer their condolences. I don't recall a single conversation, but I felt the love. Whether by adrenaline, or the love and support of friends and family, or Hannah's present spirit, I felt surprisingly bolstered. It now seemed like a larger version of the girlfriends' gathering at Grace the week before. I really don't know the source of my strength, but the fear I'd felt before the service faded with the setting sun.

As the evening came to a close and the church emptied, the gaping hole in my heart began to grow. I wondered again how I would survive without my daughter. At the same time, I couldn't get this ugly thought out of my head: *Hannah is better off dead.* Hannah had led a full, happy, and independent life before the cancer struck. The number of people who had come to celebrate her was proof of that life. I wondered if Hannah could have accepted her severely diminished level of function had she lived. Death was probably a release, a freedom for her. But I had lost her.

Our life together had been cut short. How was I going to grow old without my daughter? We were going to miss so much. Even though Hannah's spirit was still alive, how was I going to feel it directly? Could I develop the skills to contact her in the spirit world, or would I have to depend on others to deliver her messages? If I couldn't see Hannah, or hold her hand, or listen to her laugh again in this lifetime, I hoped I would come to know her spirit deep down in my bones.

Photos from Hannah's Memorial Service

Hannah at six months

Hannah with Andrew and Ryan, 1999

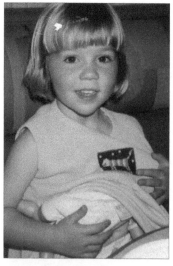

Dreaming of being a
mother, age four

Dancing girl, five years old

My beautiful girl, age eight

Hannah's ninth birthday

23

The Run of Hope

A month after Hannah died, our family participated in Seattle Children's Run of Hope, an annual fundraiser for pediatric brain cancer research that partly funds Dr. Olson's lab. This event features a five-kilometer run and a three-kilometer walk, preceded by inspirational speeches from doctors, families, and patients who are part of the childhood brain cancer world. More than half of the participating families have lost a child to these diseases. They gather support from their friends and family in memory of the kids who weren't lucky enough to survive, or who were born too soon to participate in the latest research. I had known it was too late for Hannah to benefit from the fundraiser that we'd held for Dr. Olson six months earlier. We were now part of that bigger club none of us wanted to belong to.

The year before, when Hannah was dealing with new treatment protocols following her relapse, we chose not to be part of the Run of Hope. Still not convinced that she had relapsed, I had wanted to put as much distance between the cancer world and our family as I could. But now it seemed like the right thing to do to help other kids. And we weren't alone as a newly grieving family.

I had met Kim a year earlier at a luncheon for cancer moms put on by the wives of the Seattle Seahawks. As a huge Seahawks fan thanks to Ryan, I looked forward to this special getaway, trying to dismiss the thought that this outing was for moms of the sickest kids. We were treated to lunch at a fancy restaurant in downtown Seattle. I naturally gravitated to Kim, as she was easy to talk to. I learned that her young daughter had a brain cancer more advanced than Hannah's; her child's recent terminal prognosis was reflected in her eyes. While Kim had little hope that her daughter would survive, Hannah was in better shape and I was still pursuing alternative treatments. I refused to believe that Hannah wouldn't make it. I didn't want to look the way Kim looked. In the end, Kim's daughter died one week before Hannah passed.

Between word of mouth and my CaringBridge posts, Hannah's Hopeful Hearts had amassed more than one hundred participants for its Run of Hope team. I'm certain that most folks showed up as much to support Bill and me as to give to the cause. Hauling the tent, my baked goods, and my "I can do this" mask, I boarded the 7:05 a.m. ferry with Bill on Sunday morning along with our island friends. Caroline accompanied us, bringing with her the gorgeous knitted hats—"Hannah's Hopeful Hats"—that she was making for Seattle Children's Hospital cancer patients, just as she had done for Hannah.

At Seward Park, our family pitched our event tent next to Kim's large group. Kim and I shared a hug and an unspoken understanding of our raw grief. But, organizers that we were, we soon returned to the crowds of supporters we had gathered in memory of our daughters. There wasn't time to sit down and talk about how we were each doing on the heels of their deaths. And for a while, caught up in hosting our team, I could forget that our race bibs read, *In memory of Hannah*.

I donned the event T-shirt but opted not to run that day. I wanted to walk and talk with the friends and family who had supported us for the past three years. But part of me was sad to not be running. I had completed a half-marathon with Claude in June, four months earlier. I had trained for and run it partly for my own sanity. While Hannah was sick, I'd needed to lose myself in running as a means of self-care.

I became a runner after she was born. Wanting to lose the baby weight, and inspired by Claude, who had been running for a few years, I wanted to see if I could take up this sport. Bill gave me a treadmill for Christmas, which helped me get started. With the machine parked in the living room, it was hard to come up with excuses not to exercise. I started with walking, and before long I was running short distances. Eventually I signed up for 5K and 10K races on the island, with Claude as my running partner.

When Claude ran his first marathon in Chicago in 2005, I was there to cheer him on. I was so exhilarated by the crowds, the music, and the athletes that I began to wonder if I could do it. I started training for a local marathon at the beginning of 2006. I would have been smarter to start with a half, of course, but the disciplined part of me thought that if I put in the time and the training, I could do the whole. I executed my plan perfectly, doing short runs during the week and joining Claude on the weekends for the long runs. A few weeks before the race, we completed twenty miles and shared a beer in celebration. I was ready.

But the day of the race did not go according to plan. To start with, I couldn't get my iPod to work. I tried not to panic, but I wasn't sure I could run more than twenty-six miles without my music. Andrew got it working and handed it to me at mile five, but then adrenaline probably got the better of me: with my tunes, I ran faster than my normal pace. By the midway mark I was out of gas. Claude, who had promised to stay with me no matter what, told me to take deep breaths and just walk until I could run again. For the remaining thirteen miles I could barely run. Shivering and weak from the cold, foggy weather and my lack of oxygen, I crossed the finish line with embarrassment.

Afterward, friends told me that they couldn't believe I didn't drop out of the race. But I'd said to myself before the starting gun went off, *Come hell or high water, I am going to cross that finish line, even if I have to crawl over it.* Still, it was not the race I'd envisioned or trained for.

A year later, when Hannah was diagnosed, I certainly didn't envision how her brain cancer would become our lives. Throughout my running years I had learned things that helped me through Hannah's ordeal. I learned to take it one day at a time. I learned that some days would be better than others. I learned to have patience, endurance, and resilience. I learned that training for a marathon took time, and that if I put in the work, I would be rewarded. And I learned that despite my best efforts, the outcome wouldn't always be what I hoped to achieve.

Despite the success of the race and all of the money that it raised, I left the park with an empty, unfinished feeling. Maybe it was Hannah's physical absence. Maybe it was meeting up with Kim and other moms who had also lost children this year without having time to really connect with them. Maybe it was the walk, as opposed to the adrenaline-pumping run that I was used to. Maybe it was missing a memorial announcement during the speeches for all the children who had died in the past year. Maybe I didn't yet know how to show up for a large, meaningful event without my daughter. Mostly, I had a weird, hollow feeling as we left.

I wondered why I didn't feel sadder. *Why isn't this event a tearjerker?* We were surrounded by memorials for kids lost, tributes for those still in the fight, and families searching for where to put their lost love. It wasn't actually a Sunday in the park. Even at home, I wasn't completely sad all day. I was beginning to feel Hannah's spirit filling me up and propelling me forward. I couldn't say that I was particularly joyful, but I felt a stirring from a higher place inside me.

After the Run of Hope, Bill and I took a walk in our neighborhood. We talked about the gap between the mortal and the immortal, and how if we stopped and dwelled on the fact that Hannah was no longer physically with us, it would be unbearable. Exploring the idea that her spirit was with us might explain why neither one of us was completely lost in grief. How else could I hold the box that contained her ashes and just feel numb? Maybe I was still in shock. For whatever reason, the reality of Hannah not being with us was not as painful as I had feared it would be. Maybe the tremendous shows of support at the race and her memorial, or Isabel's reported visitation, had reinforced for me that we were surrounded by love. For those experiences I was grateful.

Kim and I at the Run of Hope, 2010

Hannah's friend since preschool, Shaine, with her mom, Kathi—my friend and co-organizer—at the 2010 Run, weeks after Hannah's death

Our HHH team at the Run of Hope, 2011

Bill and I with Dr. Olson (center) and MJ and Brian at the 2013 Run

Cory and I at the Run of Hope, 2011

Claude and I at our 2006 marathon

Bill, Ryan, Andrew, and I at the Run of Hope, 2014

24

Lifelines

After the Run of Hope my calendar was wide open. There was nothing left for me to organize or plan. I didn't have a "real" job to return to, as Bill did. My work had revolved around Hannah for nearly three years. Now each day offered me a blank slate and a quiet house. Ryan had gone away to college, though fortunately only across the water to Seattle, and Andrew started his junior year of high school. I was home alone most of the day with the dogs and cats in our too-big house. Much of what happened in the following months was a blurry roller coaster of emotions. But thanks to special women in my life, I found myself enfolded in love.

When Hannah relapsed the previous year, I had flashed forward in my mind to this time when Bill and I would lose two children close together. I never imagined in my worst nightmare that Hannah and Ryan would leave weeks apart. But Ryan's departure at least gave me a job to do, and it turned out to be a surprisingly happy occasion.

The day he moved into his freshman dorm, I was surprised that my reaction was one of pride and joy, not sadness. I have always loved the job of moving. Helping Ryan pack and then move his belongings into his room gave me not only something productive to do, but also something to be excited about. We both hit it off with his roommate, Jeff, with whom he had been randomly placed. We would soon learn that Jeff had lost his mom that same summer. Their pairing seemed to be serendipitous. Finally, I could look at my firstborn and be happy for him. I didn't have to stress or worry about how Ryan would get along in college, as I had done nothing but worry about Hannah's future when she was alive. He had hoped for his life to begin again on the day that she died. Now I found myself celebrating this new chapter in Ryan's life without feeling overwhelmed by another loss.

With the work of taking Ryan to college off the list, I was back to wondering how to spend my time. A big part of me wanted to curl up into a ball, let the world go on without me, and disappear. But another part knew I needed to find a reason to get out of bed every day. A deeper part of me knew that Hannah wouldn't want her death to be the end of me. I didn't really know what I needed, but my daughter seemed to know.

Without being asked, friends began showing up to support me. I leaned hard on the core group of friends that I'd had since our children were born—Nancy, Barb, and Jen—along with my "sisters" Linda and Jeanette. They had kept me company as Hannah's condition deteriorated over the summer and waited with me for her to pass. Jen and Linda were there up to the last hours of Hannah's life, sitting in her room, reflecting on her life, and comforting me. After her death, they all showed up with flowers, lattes, wine, and hugs. They listened and wiped away my tears, but they didn't force me to talk. When I had nothing to say, they entertained me with stories of the events in their lives. With Bill so occupied at work in a busy real estate market, I don't know what I would have done without these girlfriends.

As much as they loved me, they also didn't know how I truly felt. We had weathered all kinds of storms together—illness and divorce, bumps and bruises, broken bones and broken hearts, both our own and our children's. My friends had lived through some very hard things, but none had felt the pain I was now in.

Barb's daughter, who is Ryan's age, was diagnosed with a severe disability when she was two years old. Barb has beautifully raised this girl, who requires almost constant care, and she hardly ever asks why her path is such a difficult one. Hannah, in contrast, had been healthy and independent for nine years before her diagnosis, so I struggled to adapt to her new reality and my own. Barb's daughter was happy and alive, and Barb had learned to live gracefully with her daughter's significant limitations. Hannah was stripped of her vitality and finally succumbed to her disease, and I felt robbed of my healthy girl.

We had all helped each other raise our children, so all of my friends knew Hannah and loved her like their own daughter. Yet none of them had experienced exactly what I was going through, and therefore they couldn't really know the depth of my pain. They respected that, and I was grateful for their steadfast love. Still, I felt very alone in my grief.

Suddenly, women who had lost a child began to appear at my door, as if Hannah was sending them.

First there was Stefanie, a longtime friend whom I had known since she was a teenager. Stefanie had experienced multiple miscarriages and ectopic pregnancies in recent years, including the loss of her daughter, Carey, after a preterm birth at the same time Hannah was in treatment. When we learned that Stefanie had lost her baby, Hannah asked me to help her write a sympathy card. My girl who was in love with all babies couldn't imagine losing one at birth. And it wasn't until I lost Hannah that I could begin to fathom what that loss meant to Stefanie. I knew it was a sad thing, but I couldn't really comprehend the magnitude of her grief until I was experiencing my own. Now, when Stefanie showed up at my house with lattes and bear hugs to grieve with me after Hannah's death, we bonded on a deeper level.

Stefanie also had her own knowledge about death. When she was nineteen years old, she had a near-death experience related to a rare blood malignancy. Stefanie often told me that she couldn't wait to die, knowing what's next. Now I was having those same feelings, longing to be with Hannah. Before either of us had children, we had talked a lot about what we imagined would happen in the afterlife. Now Stefanie has a whole brood of children who will greet her when she passes. Over decades of friendship, I never believed that I, too, would have a child waiting for me.

The next woman I remember showing up was Karen, who had lost her daughter, Katie, to cancer three years earlier. She said that she'd been "waiting in the wings" until I was ready to have her company. We already believed that our girls were together in heaven. Now I wanted to spend time with Karen. I looked at Karen with amazement: she had survived the loss of her daughter. I still wasn't sure that I would.

Around this time I was introduced to Molly, who would become a wise and comforting companion. She had lost her infant son in an accident decades earlier and had learned stone carving as a way to channel her grief. Even though we barely knew each other, I craved time with her because she, too, had survived many years after such a loss. When Molly offered to carve a stone for Hannah, we walked for miles on island beaches and in forests, scavenging for that special rock. (It took seven months to find it, not on a random trail, but in a place that offered a clear sign from my daughter.) Molly showed me that something creative could be sparked from my grief.

Molly would later carve a headstone for another friend's son. Robin and her husband had attended Hannah's memorial. As Robin was leaving Hannah's service, she'd said to me, "I can't imagine how you're feeling." After a month passed, she lost her twenty-one-year-old son to a sudden heart infection. At first I wondered if I had it in me to attend another funeral jam-packed with island people who had also attended Hannah's memorial. I'd only known Robin as a fellow Little League mom. But I felt an obligation to show up, as she had done for me.

When Bill and I attended their full-house service, another friend sat next to me and explained the traditions of the Jewish funeral. Eschewing tradition, Robin wore white, as I had at Hannah's service. I watched the surviving sister walking down the aisle to her seat, hanging on to her older brother. The siblings were similar in age to Ryan and Andrew, and I wondered how distraught they must be at this sudden loss. I thought, *What's harder for siblings and parents, experiencing a sudden death or having a long time to prepare for it?* Of course, neither is better. In the end, we'd both lost our precious children.

After the service, a smaller contingent of family and friends processed to the cemetery for the burial, which typically takes place within days of the death. I was scared to show up to this intimate and emotional setting, but I chose to go. It felt as if a magnet were pulling me to this woman and her grieving family. One of the main purposes of the grave-side ceremony is to help the loved one find their final resting place. This symbolic act involves placing earth in the grave. I stood in the back of the smaller crowd, holding Bill's hand and not knowing if I could find the strength to participate. The sound alone was jarring. But something pushed me forward. I think it was Hannah nudging me to take up the shovel and place dirt on the coffin. After I took my turn, I walked up to Robin and hugged her. I could only say, "I'm sorry." But at that moment, looking in her eyes, I knew we were now more than bleacher friends.

Much to my amazement, another bereaved mom sought me out shortly after Robin buried her son. Bainbridge is small, and it didn't take long for Mary Jane to find me. She and her husband had just moved to the island. They had heard through the real estate community that our family had lost a daughter to a brain tumor—just as they had. My heart went out to MJ, who had struggled to get pregnant with her only child and then lost her in such a tragic way. Between our common trag-edies, her honest and dark sense of humor, and her couple years' expe-rience with grief, we became fast friends.

MJ was also fascinated by the afterlife, so she shared resources on grieving with me, including books by medium George Anderson. After Isabel's visitation with Hannah, I was curious about individuals who could contact the dead. Now, thanks to MJ, I began to ponder the idea of meeting with George to contact Hannah.

A couple months later I met Teri, whose adult son had died in an acci-dent. I didn't know it when we first met, but Teri would complete our club of bereaved moms.

I was amazed by the appearance of these bereaved women in my life right after Hannah's death. They seemed to be divinely sent, or perhaps even Hannah-sent. I hadn't looked for them, but they had found me.

I was so grateful to have these new friends. I hadn't been particu-larly interested in joining a ready-made support group for bereaved parents such as the Compassionate Friends. While I know that group has benefited some parents, I was glad that my group of grieving moms happened organically, without requiring me to summon up the courage to meet with a group of strangers. These women wouldn't replace my old friends, but they offered something that my other friends couldn't: understanding of what it's like to lose a child.

People who didn't have that experience couldn't understand how we felt or what we were going through. I found an immediate, raw, and honest connection with these bereaved mothers. Not everyone would want to hear the things we talked about: What clothes did you dress your child in before they were carted off to the funeral home? How was it to gaze upon their face for the last time? What mystical signs have you received from your dead child? How do you respond when others ask, "How many children do you have?"

I hoped that we could learn something from each other about love and loss, something that would help get us through the unbearable sadness. But at least we could witness our individual grieving without giving anyone a timetable or any judgment around how they were doing it. In her book *Bearing the Unbearable*, Dr. Joanne Cacciatore says, "I reflected on a mysterious quality of grief: when we look into the eyes of another, someone who has known suffering, without a word we know that they know, and there is something painfully restorative in that mutual recognition."

Early on, my new bereaved friends met often, individually and collectively. We took lots of long walks and had beer and wine at our "crappy hours." As time went on, we attempted to write in groups, although we accomplished more support and talking than writing. We shared books on grief or for needed escape. We even took short vacations together. These women became my lifelines.

I needed them as much as I needed my long-term friends. I clung to the women who fed me, literally and emotionally. My true friends loved all of me, even my raw edges. When I was with them, I didn't have to pretend I was fine. I didn't have to fake my emotions. They cried alongside me. We laughed together. They kept me alive.

Over the months after Hannah's death, I whittled down my friends to two groups: my core group of old friends and my "friends with dead kids." I used my "I get to do whatever I damn well please" card to let go of women who didn't feel authentic to me. I divorced a couple of friends I didn't feel comfortable with, either because I had to put on an act with them or because they smothered me with their grief around Hannah. One woman even said that she felt more loss over Hannah's death than her own father's. I believe her grief was genuine, but it didn't help me to hear about it. It felt as though she were somehow trying to steal my grief over my beloved daughter.

Being able to choose and claim my real friends became a surprising gift after losing Hannah. These women sustained me through those chilly fall months.

As the holidays approached, I worried less about what I was going to do with myself. I had to get out of bed in the morning: my calendar was filling up with coffee dates and walks with friends. I was mercifully distracted with these outings, which helped me to stop dwelling on Hannah's final days. For the most part, my time was my own, to spend as I chose. And I needed that freedom.

I had lived through three years of trauma. I had used up all of myself in caring for Hannah. I had mothered her from the moment she was conceived, including hospitalization during my difficult pregnancy. The last three years of her life took everything out of me. Now I was the one needing mothering. Since my own mother was no longer living, my friends stepped into that role. Almost all of them were moms themselves. I needed them to show up for me with their caring and nurturing, just as other women had shown up for my mom at the end of her life. My battered heart needed healing. In my grief, and with the support of those friends, I found my heart opening and softening, much as it had when I became a new mother. Those women were a big part of why I was still standing.

Jen, Nancy, Barb, and I
on the beach at La Push,
November 2010

On vacation with my friends with dead
kids: Robin, Karen, Teri, and Stefanie

Birthday with friends Jeanette, Nancy,
Kathi, Stefanie, and Jen

Linda and I on vacation, 2018

25

A Hawaiian Christmas

Before I knew it, the holidays were upon me. I hadn't had another sign from Hannah, so the warm fuzzy feeling of knowing her spirit was alive was fading with the diminishing light of the coming winter solstice. We survived Thanksgiving, thanks to the company of Jeanette, Linda, and the cousins at home. But I dreaded the first Christmas without Hannah. I knew early on that I didn't want to be home for her favorite holiday. I wouldn't be able to look at the decorations, the stockings, the manger she always erected, or anything else that said Hannah to me. We needed a different plan.

A client of Bill's generously offered her condo in Hawaii for the winter break. As much as I appreciated that gift, I was hesitant at first to go back to the place where we had vacationed with the kids. Our last time on Maui was months before Hannah was diagnosed, and she had been fully active—swimming, playing tennis, and dragging me to various shopping venues. But, ultimately, getting out of town and staying in a wonderful place beat out the idea of staying at home.

Maui turned out to be a good change of scenery. Every day was picture perfect. When we got off the plane, we were met with warm, perfumed breezes. The condo was luxurious and beautiful, with a hilltop view of the ocean. We enjoyed meals outside on the patio, next to wide-open stretches of rolling grass. I took lots of walks by myself along the beach and on trails that wound around the seaside rocks.

One morning, I woke before the rest of the family to see a stunning rainbow directly across the water. Hannah and I had never talked about rainbows, but in my heart I took it as a sign that she was with me. I was looking for signs of her everywhere. At our favorite local breakfast place, I noticed a butterfly lighting on a window next to me. I convinced myself it was another sign of Hannah's presence. I was doing my darn best to believe that she was with us on that trip.

One of my favorite parts of the vacation was Christmas morning. I had not been looking forward to it, but we did not do any of our traditional Christmas things, so it was better than I'd expected. Normally I went all out with gifts, decorations, and food. Away from home, I didn't have to do any of it. In lieu of big gifts, we had asked everyone to put something small and inexpensive in each other's stockings. Now, instead of me creating Christmas, we were all responsible for it. I loved discovering what Ryan and Andrew had come up with as small stocking stuffers. A simple brunch on our patio replaced the typical large holiday spread. I got a glimpse of how our family could create new traditions rather than repeat old ones that would have had me missing Hannah more.

Still, despite the beautiful place and the new memories, I couldn't get Hannah out of my mind as the week progressed. I continued trying to walk off my grief, as I had been doing on Bainbridge, but had very little success. The condo was near the place where we had vacationed with Hannah. Walking past the beach, the pools, the tennis courts, and the putt-putt course where she had played was heart-wrenching. I was so sad that this was our new reality as a family.

To make matters worse, Andrew remained disengaged from our activities. While Ryan and Bill boogie boarded in the surf, Andrew sat on the beach with me. It would have helped if he'd talked to me, though in fact I wasn't much for conversation. But other than when we dined, Andrew seemed to fade into the background. And I was fading into my own island of despair.

I felt a growing separation from Bill and the boys. Bill was sad, but he didn't have the time or space at home to explore his loss. As the sole family provider, he'd had to get back to work. He couldn't spend whole days walking and thinking about his daughter or keeping company with caring friends. He and the boys hadn't been through as much trauma as I had with Hannah. I knew they didn't love her any less, but they hadn't witnessed, as I had, all of the brutal suffering that she had experienced. The time Hannah and I had spent together made us extremely close. Even though Hannah was a child, we had developed a profound and intimate bond with each other. Now it was gone. All of us were dealing with some level of grief, but it didn't feel equal.

During the trip, it was hard for me and Bill to talk about Hannah. Sharing our sadness felt too painful. We were trying to get away from the awful memories of the past three years. There were too many hellish events from her cancer ordeal, not to mention the pain of remembering who she was before she got sick. Bill told me later that he was afraid to fully face his loss.

Since Hannah died, we'd been seeing our hospice social worker, Laura, for bereavement counseling. Several people had cautioned us that most couples don't survive the death of a child. We didn't want to be that statistic, so we chose to talk about it with a counselor. Bill and I liked Laura and felt comfortable with her, which doesn't always happen in couples counseling. But on the trip we took a vacation from counseling topics.

Still, we knew we'd have to learn to be a married couple again. We'd spent very little time alone together since Hannah got sick. I had often been away with her while Bill was home, working or with Ryan and Andrew. When I needed a break from the hospital, he spelled me. When I wasn't with Hannah, I'd wanted to reconnect with the boys. I could probably count on one hand the number of times Bill and I'd been alone or out together since she was diagnosed.

With Hannah's nightmare illness as a prime example, Bill and I learned that we are good in a crisis. We work well together. We know how to adapt, seek help, adjust our priorities, and share the load. We can be present for difficult conversations. Bill and I had been with Hannah when she went in for neurosurgery, when her head was screwed to the table for radiation, when she heard the cancer was back, when she was airlifted, when we signed the DNR paper, and when she took her last breath. We make a good team when life is very, very hard.

But when the focus is just on us—when there isn't an imminent emergency—we tend to retreat to our corners and wait for the next battle. Sometimes we can be too self-sufficient for our own good. With the cumulative stress, we'd also forgotten how to have fun together. We could lean on each other in the midst of a life-or-death situation, but ordinary life had become a challenge. Now that Hannah was gone and the crisis had passed, we needed to learn how to be a regular couple again. In Hawaii, Bill and I took some time alone, but mostly I was by myself, lost in my own grief. I sought the comfort of solitude over togetherness.

I'd brought several books on grief and the afterlife, since I had become obsessed with where Hannah was and how I could live without her. In Nicholas Wolterstorff's book *Lament for a Son*, I was struck by a passage that perfectly captured my feelings: "Sometimes I think that happiness is over for me. I look at photos of the past and immediately comes the thought: that's when we were still happy. But I can still laugh, so I guess that isn't quite it. Perhaps what's over is happiness as the fundamental tone of my existence. Now sorrow is that. Sorrow is no longer the islands but the sea."

I was being engulfed by sadness. I knew that Bill and the boys were sad about Hannah, but we weren't in the same place with our grief. Getting through the first holidays without her felt harder for me. Bill was happy for a break from work. Ryan loved being on a tropical beach vacation. And Andrew was content to have a break from his life. I mostly felt lonely for Hannah.

Our Christmas getaway was a mixed bag of new traditions and uncomfortable loneliness. On a deepening level, I was struggling to know how to have a life without my daughter. I hoped that someday these feelings would change. I hoped I would someday experience Hannah with me, as a vital part of my spiritual life. But as the year wound down, I missed her with all of my being.

Christmas brunch in Hawaii

Dinner out on Maui

26

George

Back at home from Hawaii and facing the short, dark days of winter, I struggled to crawl out from under the covers of my sad existence. The one thing that offered me a bit of light was the possibility of connecting to Hannah through George Anderson. For months I had devoured George's books, including *We Don't Die, George Anderson's Lessons from the Light*, and *Walking in the Garden of Souls*. I found such comfort in the stories he told. I believed him to be a credible medium. He wasn't as well known as others in the field, but he did have a history working with Dr. Elisabeth Kübler-Ross. I grew determined to meet with him. With Bill on board, and hoping that we might be able to communicate with Hannah, we made an appointment to meet George.

In the spring of 2011 Bill and I flew to New York for our session with him. When we arrived at the suburban Long Island hotel where we would meet with him the following day, we were filled with nervous excitement. After checking into our room, Bill and I sat in the lobby, hoping to catch sight of George walking out of the conference room where his sessions were held. Just as we were about to give up, we saw a short-statured man briskly walk out of the room and exit the hotel, followed by a couple of women. This glimpse of the man we presumed was George was so brief, I was immediately disappointed. In the back of my mind, I had hoped he would notice us, get a quick message from Hannah, and then come over to talk with us. We would have to wait for our appointed time.

The next day dragged on forever as we waited for the four o'clock session. We walked and walked, trying to kill time. I had the strangest anticipatory feeling, almost as if we were expecting a baby. I was convinced that Hannah would appear to George and that it would be a rebirth of sorts.

At last it was time. We were escorted into a conference room and took our seats at the end of a long conference table. The businesslike setting was a striking contrast to what I hoped would be an otherworldly experience. My heart pounded in my chest.

George sat on the other end of the table with pen and notebook in hand. Dressed neatly and casually, he had a strong New York accent with a rather abrupt, serious manner. There were few pleasantries, as George insists upon working with minimal knowledge of whom he is sitting with. He only knew that we were a couple and that we were present to hear from someone who had died.

When our session began, George looked not at Bill and me, but rather at the wall. He began drawing quick circles on his pad of paper. I knew from George's books that he uses this automatic writing technique to connect with souls in the hereafter, as he calls it.

He first told us that there were many souls gathering in the conference room. I held my breath, hoping Hannah would be the one who stepped forward and not our parents or other relatives who had passed years earlier. He started by saying, "They're talking about the loss of a child. Actually, they're talking about the loss of two. One child you knew, the other you didn't." Tears rolled down my face, as George had just confirmed the loss of Hannah and of the baby I'd miscarried the year before Ryan was born. George informed us that the baby we lost was a boy and that the child we knew in this life was a girl. It was comforting in a strange way to learn the sex of the first baby, but it was also more proof to me that George was truly listening to the souls who had gathered around us.

George then focused on Hannah, who had stepped forward in his mind's eye to speak with him. At times he summarized what she was telling him, and at other times he directly quoted what she was saying. He began by telling us that Hannah apologized for her death. She said, "Now that it's all over, I'm fine and back to my old self." George said that she was joking with him, as she added, "I'm surprised I made it as far as I did." George told us that she wasn't supposed to be "there" (in heaven) yet. And then Hannah said, "If I had gone there earlier, they would have sent me back. I made it as far as I could until it was realized that it was my time."

George related that it was just a question of time before Hannah would welcome us over there. He said, "Someday when you meet her there in the joyful reunion, it will seem as if she left in one moment and you followed in the next. And everything will be clearly understood."

George described Hannah's life as courageous, enduring, and per-severing—all words that were very much true in her last three years. Hannah said, "I'll admit it wasn't fun. But I dealt with it as courageously as I could. Don't think I didn't have a fulfilling life. I did." When Hannah talked about having fulfilled her purpose, it was confirmation of what I had contemplated with Steve Forrest. She then stated, "I'm all right, and in a happy, safe place. I'm fine." George told us that she also expressed gratitude to us for walking with her through the experience. (He had not yet discerned that she died of an illness.)

One of the surest signs we had that George was communicating with Hannah was how her personality came through as he reported on what she told him. At times she seemed to be challenging him; he picked up on her strong-willed nature, saying, "I've got myself a feisty gal! She's not being mean; she has to come in that way because it's how you know and love her." I certainly knew and loved my opinionated, stubborn daughter.

In surprising news, given her positive attitude, Hannah told George that she hadn't been the happiest person. She said, "Many things I might have kept to myself. I tried my best to keep on a happy face, but I wasn't the happiest on the inside." We realized that Hannah was refer-ring to times when she was sick and didn't let us know how she was really feeling. We guessed that she was trying to protect us from how bad she felt as she endured one torturous treatment after another, all the while missing her normal life.

George said, "She wants to make sure you know that as parents you did not fail." Hannah said, "You did the best you could." After all of the treatment, the recovery, the ups and downs, and the final loss, these words were comforting to hear, even though we'd also learned how unhappy she'd been. There was my honest daughter.

Before George figured out that she had died of a brain tumor, she reported to him several times, "Tell them I'm walking fine . . . back to normal." Since Hannah had had to regain her ability to walk after the initial brain surgery, this was strong evidence that George was indeed talking with her. We knew that for a girl who excelled at dance, not being able to walk, run, or move gracefully had been very frustrating. George backed this up by saying, "There was a hindrance to her independence, an unpredictability of it."

Hannah then spent a great deal of time describing to George the symptoms and origin of her illness. She went into so much detail about the genesis of her cancer that I later wondered if she was trying to teach the doctors and researchers, coming from a place of knowing more than they might, about the potential cause and cure of her brain cancer. One of her doctors was gracious enough to read this portion of the transcript. He didn't find the information helpful, but I was grateful that he at least read it.

Hannah concluded by saying, "I'm proud to say that I gave it a run for its money. . . . I wasn't going to lay back. . . . If I was going to go there, okay, but I was going to go kicking and screaming."

She told George that she knew she was going to die and that she didn't suffer at the end. Even though she had been nonverbal and semi-comatose in the last weeks of her life, she told him that she knew we were there, talking to her and holding her hand, waiting for the inevitable. This was very comforting for us to hear. We'd had no idea at the time whether she was still in pain. Because we were especially troubled by the fact that we hadn't talked openly with her about her impending death, Hannah seemed to be trying to relieve us of our worry and guilt. George interpreted what she was trying to communicate by saying, "You and the rest of the family and friends made a great contributing factor to help her to reach her spiritual triumph."

Hannah also thanked us for her memorial service. She "called out"— which according to George meant that she was sending love and greetings—to her cousin Chris. Since she had just thanked us for the service, I assumed she was thanking him for his beautiful performance of "Hallelujah." And she gave thanks for the planting in her remembrance. George said he saw a tree shoot up in front of him. We had just planted a cherry tree at Grace Church in Hannah's memory two weeks before.

Hannah further expressed gratitude for the tremendous support she was given when she was sick. "Not only family, but so many friends were there for me," she said, joking, "We can't call out a roll call—we'll be here till five a.m." George commented that it sounded like Hannah had a really sincere and compassionate support system. It's true: a huge number of her friends and ours supported us. "There was a tremendous show-up at her funeral," said George. "Even you're surprised," Hannah said, "even I'm surprised. . . . People came that to this day you didn't even know who they were."

George said that Hannah also expressed appreciation for the many people who had done kindnesses on her behalf. He said that we may or may not know about these acts, but she knew the good intentions behind them. In his books, George often speaks of how prayer and good and loving actions done in a loved one's honor benefit not only those on Earth but also those who have passed.

Toward the end of the session, George told me that he was seeing the Blessed Mother behind me. I knew that during his readings he often saw saints who had meanings either for him or for the person sitting with him. George said, "One bereaved mother to another." He said that the presence of Mary had nothing to do with religion or my beliefs but that "only someone who has gone through it or is going through it will understand how you feel." To me this message was a confirmation of all the grieving moms surrounding me. I believe Hannah was symbolically conveying her greatest wish to me through George. She was not only giving me the sign I had asked for, but also, by connecting me with others who were going through the same thing, giving me what she knew I needed the most: comfort. From one bereaved mother to another.

I knew our session was winding down, but I wanted to hear more. Before we said goodbye to George, Hannah announced, "Katie is here!" At first I wondered whether Hannah was talking about our old black lab, Katy, who had died years before, or the girl who had passed before her. Hannah spent a lot of time talking about Katie with George, and he worked so hard to determine who this person was; we decided that she was referring to the girl who looked like Courtney, whom she had seen before she died, and not our beloved family pet.

Before we met with George, I had hoped to bring back news to one of my bereaved women friends as well. Now that Hannah seemed to be directing me, through George, to other mothers who had also lost a child, I was excited to call Karen after our session and tell her that Hannah and Katie were together. Although I'm sure Karen would have rather received the news when she wasn't standing in the aisle at Costco.

At the end of the session, George said that Hannah embraced Bill and me with love and "called out" to her family, including her girlfriends and "sisters." She said, "Tell them not to be frightened by what's happened. Because I'm young, and the next thing they know they see my dead body.... It scares them.... There's nothing to be afraid of. They'll find out for themselves one day, but I can kind of guarantee them now there's nothing to fear but fear itself.... They think it's just so final that I didn't get a chance at my life."

"It's the life in your years that count, not the other way around," George commented. Hannah's call to not be afraid was the second time we'd heard this message from her. The first was during her visit with Isabel.

Finally she said, "My life goes on here." George reported that Hannah was around as a guardian angel. "No big surprise," he said, smiling. In his books, George often talks about how the journey we're on continues after our physical death. He told us that souls have many different jobs. Back home, when they listened to the recording, Caroline and Ryan were deeply touched to hear that Hannah had been acting as their guardian angel.

We left our meeting with George feeling that we'd heard from Hannah and she was alive and well in spirit. Immediately afterward, we went out to dinner to celebrate. It was as if we were newly expecting or had just given birth, our joy was so great. Over dinner at a nearby Italian restaurant, we replayed all that we had heard. Back in our hotel room, I listened to my recording of the session twice, just to make sure I hadn't missed anything. I would play the tape over and over in the weeks to come, until I had practically memorized it. I couldn't hear enough from Hannah.

The session was further proof that Hannah was indeed present, very much alive, just as we had heard from Isabel. I was encouraged to keep replacing my images of her dying with images of her continuing life, focusing on the beautiful memories of my daughter and not on the suffering she had endured with her illness. I still longed to be with her, but hearing again that she was happy and at peace, I felt urged to look at what was left for me to do and how I could live my life without her.

The meeting with George and Hannah tempered the sadness I'd been feeling for months. It was reassuring to hear that Hannah was happy, back to her old self, and watching over us. And it was especially comforting to know that she was not alone, nor was she afraid.

These statements may sound trite or general, but the personal details that George discerned in the communication were too real to not be true, to not be coming from Hannah. I will be forever grateful that MJ introduced me to George. From the start of the session, he offered up definitive proof of his contact with Hannah by telling us that we had lost two children—a fact that not many people knew. Now I can take comfort knowing that the son we never met is with the daughter we loved in this world.

Bill and I with Buddy and Moose at Hannah's cherry tree

27

A New Home

The session with George sparked a long overdue new chapter for Bill and me. Over dinner after our time with him, we began to envision a different place to live. We had wanted to move from the five-bedroom home where Hannah died, but we either couldn't find the right place or felt that it was premature. Now we were inspired to consider a house right next door to the home where our kids grew up. Bill and I felt that Hannah, through George, had given us the idea for where to live next.

After we returned from our trip, we went directly to the owners of the house we had begun to imagine ourselves buying. Lynne and Carter had become good friends over the years. Our kids grew up with their daughter, Alli, who naturally became their big sister, babysitter, and backyard baseball player. Hannah and Alli were especially close. As Hannah got older, the girls had endless fun watching movies, having sleepovers, going shopping, eating out, and arguing over whether Sleeping Beauty should be dressed in blue (Hannah) or pink (Alli). When Hannah was sick and Alli was finishing law school in Seattle, Alli made a point of coming to see her little sister every chance she could. Despite their thirteen-year age difference, they were very close.

Bill had always admired the view and the setting of our friends' house overlooking Port Madison bay. Bill is an architect by training and had been drawing up plans for it in his head for years. I had sworn to him that if we were to own this 1860s mill house, I could never tear it down. In yet another example of serendipity, Lynne and Carter said that they were ready to sell their old house and were excited to learn we were interested. They gave us their blessing to do whatever we wanted with it. In the same weekend that we reached a deal with our friends, we sold our house and found a rental to live in while our new home was being remodeled. I was grateful for the ease of these transactions; it seemed our move was meant to be. We gave Hannah most of the credit for being the catalyst.

One particular moment convinced me we were making the right move. I had spent a lot of time at the neighbors' house and thought I knew it well. Lynne and Carter were also amazing gardeners, so over the years we had shared plants and veggies from our respective yards. But on the day we went to talk to them about possibly buying their home, I noticed something in their backyard that I'd never seen before.

I walked out the kitchen door and saw a large rock sitting in Lynne's rose garden. I turned to Bill and said, "Look! It's Hannah's rock!" For months I'd been walking with my friend Molly, looking for a special rock that she would carve for us. This one wasn't particularly attractive, but it had a flat top and was big enough to sit on. It seemed to be saying to me, *Take a seat. You've found your new home. Love, Hannah.*

The rock sat prominently in a part of the yard that would eventually become Hannah's garden. In this enclosed space, I imagined adding my favorite roses, lavender, and perennials to some established plantings. I also pictured mosaic garden stones lining the brick pathway. On the one-year anniversary of Hannah's death, friends and family would gather at our rental house to create these stones, which I would later place in her garden. I thanked Hannah for yet another sign.

A year after we'd rebuilt and moved into our new bay-view home, Hannah sent a more direct sign that we were in the right place. Outside her garden I'd planted vegetables and sunflowers, as I always did. But sometime around June I noticed a green stalk growing right next to the brick pathway in the middle of Hannah's garden. Fortunately, I didn't assume it was a weed and pull it, but rather kept watering it, wondering if it could actually be what it looked like, a sunflower. Leave it to Hannah to plunk something that signified her spirit right in the middle of her very own garden!

When the sunflower bloomed on what would have been Hannah's fifteenth birthday, it felt like a miracle. I don't think I could have planned this sunny "Hello!" from my girl if I'd tried. I was also overjoyed that Alli was with me in the garden to witness the bloom. Of course, a bird probably dropped the sunflower seed, but what was remarkable was that it grew up in the very center of Hannah's garden. It grew to a shorter height than most sunflowers but had a gigantic head. To us it appeared to stand as tall as Hannah had in the final years of her life. I could say that, characteristic of a Sun-ruled Leo, she was almost showing off with that flower in her birth month of August. Here was Hannah, standing in her garden as the sunflower, a symbol of life, happiness, energy, and vitality.

While she never lived in our new home, her spirit found a way to put down roots there. However Hannah delivered this sign to Earth, I was grateful for the birthday greeting. Many of my friends know that I dread the month of August. My own birthday is in the middle of the month, surrounded by Hannah's birth and death dates. Three years after her death, I was doing better but still having days that felt pretty dark, especially on her birthday. And now here she was in her garden, reminding me to turn my head to the sun, and to life, the way sunflowers do.

I was grateful that Hannah had planted the seed for Bill and me to create a new home. After we met with George, we had been so overcome with joy that a new conversation sparked between us, replacing the one that went, "How are we going to continue on without our daughter?" with "Should we find somewhere new to live?" Moving had felt too hard to face at first. I hadn't been ready to go through Hannah's things and pack up her room for good, since she'd never have another bedroom in our house. What I finally realized was that while Hannah didn't have a room in our new house, she would be right there with us every day.

Lynne and Carter's old mill
house

The house as it looks today

Ryan, Bill, Andrew, and I with
the miracle sunflower

Hannah's garden with mosaic
stones lining the path

Mosaic party on the anniversary of Hannah's death with
Stefanie, MJ, Sarah, Linda, and Caroline

28

The Light and the Dark

I just want my daughter back. There was a time after Hannah died when I didn't care if I lived or died. I had never been as close to another human being, even Bill, as I had to my daughter. Her three-year struggle only brought us closer. The depth of my grief was equal to the depth of my love for her. And even though we had a lot of good in our lives, I still struggled a year after she'd passed. It was hard to escape the feeling that I didn't want a life without Hannah.

Between the fall of 2011 and the summer of 2012, we lived in the rental house while our new home was being built. The temporary place was conveniently located within walking distance of town and of the high school for Andrew. It was a welcome novelty to not always need to drive to get somewhere. The home, a fifties-era rambler, wasn't really my style. But it did have a nice deck off the back with a hot tub and a view of the water. We lived with the basic necessities, putting a lot of our furniture and household items in storage until the new house was ready. Living in this bare-bones strange place, without a room for Hannah, probably contributed to my feeling out of sorts. No matter how many things there were to look forward to, my heart was numb.

I had many things to be grateful for that could distract me from missing Hannah, but I found it difficult to focus on them. The dream house that Bill had finally gotten to design was under construction. Alexis and Adam had their first child, an event that Hannah had dreamed about. Ryan was thriving in college and was close enough to come home every month or so. Even Andrew seemed to have a new lease on life, as he had begun exercising and eating better. Still, despite all the good happening around me, a dark cloud lingered.

In the quiet times, when it was just me home alone, I could easily fall into a deep, depressing hole. Despite Hannah's visit with Isabel and her messages through George, despite the excitement over the new house and the companionship of my newfound friends, despite feeling surprisingly okay on the one-year anniversary of her death, and even despite the birth of Adam's healthy baby girl, I was having a harder time.

My mood was as variable as the moon. Some days I could be fairly productive and relatively happy. But, more often, I lived in a confused fog, wondering if and how to get myself out of it. In the morning when I journaled, I contemplated the same things over and over—what I was going to do with my day, how I was going to find some energy, or how I was going to quit feeling like Eeyore. Some days I could distract myself with a friend or a dog walk or some family gathering; other days I lay on the couch, eating popcorn in front of a movie I'd seen twenty times, not caring if I wasted another day. More times than I dared to admit, I didn't want to keep living.

I couldn't imagine living the rest of my life without Hannah. The relief that her suffering was over, coupled with the knowledge we had received that she was at peace, had been replaced with a sad longing. In January I wrote, *Lately, a deep sadness has settled into my being, my new way of being in my new life without Hannah. I am now defined by a gaping hole in my heart. I know I'm not alone but it often feels that way. No matter who I am with or what I am doing, I usually feel separate from those people or that activity.*

I had heard from other bereaved moms that the second year after you lose someone precious was harder than the first. I was beginning to know it. Another mom who was further down the road in her own grief was Claire, the woman who helped me create the mosaic stone project for Hannah's garden. She had lost her two daughters in a plane crash over a decade earlier and had established her mosaic studio as a nurturing place for people to heal. She sent me these words that perfectly described how I'd been feeling:

> Grief makes us lonely. There is a certain kind of loneliness that is created when someone very dear to us dies. Lonely in a deep untouchable way. We feel it even when we are surrounded by people we love. It is unaffected by wonderful things that might be happening around us. It's as if time freezes at that moment of loss and we split. Many of us live with an ever present loneliness and ache for not only those who died, but also for our own selves, the part of us that is forever lost in that other time-stopped world.

I didn't know who I was without Hannah. I had primarily been a mother for two decades. But that role was quickly diminishing, as Andrew would be launching in less than a year. I hated my nearly empty nest. I was now also a grandmother, but I didn't feel like one. Adam and Alexis's daughter, Penelope, was born eerily close to the anniversary of Hannah's death. With their family in Los Angeles, we seldom saw them, so I didn't feel connected to my new granddaughter, nor did I feel as close to them as I had when Hannah was still alive. I felt too young and too cheated to be a grandmother already. I still wanted to raise my daughter.

In October I offered to help take care of Penelope when Adam finished paternity leave and went back to work. I was scheduled to go by myself, but since I'd raised three kids, I didn't think helping Alexis take care of an infant would be a big deal. On the day I was to fly out, I arrived at the airport and got sick. I've never had a panic attack, but I experienced shortness of breath, nausea, and increasing anxiety. I walked up to the gate agent and said, "I can't get on this flight." I turned around, got back on the light rail, took the ferry home, and crawled into bed. When I called Alexis to tell her I couldn't come because I was sick, I felt guilty. I stayed in bed for a long time thinking about how I had let her down. I had not made good on my promise. But I also don't know that she or Adam understood the depth of my grief.

Without Hannah, I felt alone most of the time. Even though I had great friends and a lot of freedom to do as I pleased, I felt adrift. Bill was busy at work, trying to reestablish his real estate practice while also functioning as the contractor on our house project. When he was home, I didn't feel connected to him. He seemed to be caught up in his various jobs, leaving me to think about our daughter. A lot of the time I found him annoying and preoccupied—whether or not he deserved my judgment.

When I confided these feelings to Isabel, she told me, "I've been trying to connect with Hannah on and off for the past few weeks. I've had no success except for one brief communication. I told her that you and Bill needed her, and she said, 'They need each other.'" Hannah was right about that, but I didn't know how to close the gap that divided us.

We were still seeing Laura, our bereavement counselor, every week. In her presence we did pretty well at sharing our feelings. But when she wasn't there, we stopped communicating about anything sensitive. Bill said, "I can't be where you are, sitting in your grief. It would kill me." It was hard to know if our difficulty getting along was a fundamental problem or just the grief talking. Regardless, we were not on the same page.

Kathi, another close confidant of mine, also felt a strong psychic connection to Hannah. She shared with me a vivid dream she'd had. Hannah was among a group of people in the house that seemed to be our rental home. She sat at a counter with other young people, perhaps including Katie. An older woman with white hair and blue eyes was among the many elderly folks present. This woman approached Kathi and put her hands on her face so she could look clearly into her eyes. When Kathi and I talked about her dream, it seemed significant that among other friends and older folks, probably distant relatives, my mom, the white-haired woman with blue eyes, was there with Hannah.

It was comforting to hear from my friend that my mom was probably with my daughter. Still, I wanted to be the one with her.

Hannah had come to me several times in my dreams, always at different ages. Sometimes the image of her was clear and comforting, as when she gave me a hug and I could actually feel her touch; other times I would just get brief, vague glimpses of her. Such dreams usually left me wanting more.

Occasionally, I would get a quick greeting from Hannah. The signs usually came through music. One day that fall, I had gone to Seattle with a friend with whom I used to play music. Suzanne invited me to a local television show's taping of the psychic James Van Praagh. Since we had heard a lot from Hannah through George Anderson, I was hopeful that we might hear from her again, even though it was in a public setting. On the ferry ride over, Suzanne told me that she had dreamed of Hannah, who told her I would know she was with me when I heard Katy Perry's music. That message seemed pretty random. At the studio in Seattle, Hannah didn't come through during James's presentation. But she did during a commercial break, when Perry's song "Firework" came on over the speakers. Suzanne and I just looked at each other and smiled.

Back home that same day, I felt as if Hannah was trying to reach out to me again through music. I had set my iPod on shuffle while I was making dinner. Every single song that popped up was a Hannah favorite, once again including "Firework." I had goose bumps. Unfortunately, as real as these brief contacts with Hannah felt, they didn't last.

Unfinished business also added stress to my despairing mental state. Building a house comes with millions of large and small decisions, and I felt hard-pressed to make any of them. I was relieved that Bill handled the bulk of the big ones, but I didn't want the finished home to be entirely of his choosing. I was too stubborn for that. But all of the smaller details, from paint colors to lighting to fixtures, overwhelmed me. It took me months, along with the help of a designer, before I could begin to make those choices. Our inspired home had become a stressful undertaking.

Another source of anxiety was my relationship with my brother. The reality of Claude's departure from our lives was finally catching up to me. I was angry and sad about when and how he had left his own family, let alone me. When I finally got up the courage to write to him about how I was feeling, he said, "I'm surprised it took you so long to tell me." It would be months before we would finally sit down and talk face-to-face. I knew he had to live his own life, but he had indirectly dealt me another loss. The absence of the brother who had always been there for me was not helping my depression. I missed my running buddy.

I struggled to find a reason to live, a purpose. Without a clear idea of what I should do next, I did nothing. My heart and my head battled over whether to have faith and give it time, or to just give in to the darkness. I seriously questioned whether I should even still be here or not. I indulged in fantasies about how I could end my life. I could die from exposure, an overdose, an accident. I joked with some of my bereaved friends about how we could end our lives to be with our children again and escape the endless pain. A couple of us even made pacts to not jump off an island bridge unless we took the others along. I'm not sure if that talk was all in jest, if there was some real truth in it, or if there was an unspoken guarantee that if one of us had really reached the end of our rope, we would let someone know who could prevent it. In any case, it was easy to indulge in such thoughts as a means of stopping the hurt.

Ultimately, I knew I could never end my life. I wouldn't ever do that to my husband, my kids, my friends, or Hannah. I couldn't cause them more pain than they'd already experienced. And I'd probably never get up the courage to act.

Astrology confirmed that I was in the midst of a lonely, dark time. I was aware that Saturn was moving over the moon in my birth chart during this bleak period. This planetary movement hitting a key part of my chart reflected what was happening in my life. Saturn correlates with endings and limitations; the moon represents feelings and family. These two dissimilar energies may offer an explanation for my defeatist and self-destructive ideas during that time. The harsh reality of Saturn—in my increasing knowledge that Hannah was gone—had a depressive effect on my mood. It also reflected my awareness of the losses and new structure of my family. And while it didn't feel good, it explained why I preferred to be alone, why I doubted myself, and why I thought about ending my life to stop the heartache. The good news about this critical period in my life was that it was finite. This planetary interaction lasted roughly from December 2011 through March 2012. It's easier for me now to look back and understand why I was having such a hard time. It was a necessary phase.

In the months ahead, I would have to find my way out of the darkness. I wasn't sure how, but I wouldn't give up. I had to recapture the joy I'd felt at learning that Hannah was still alive in spirit. I had to find a new purpose. I had to focus on things to look forward to in my life, and the things I had to be grateful for. I had to find reasons to live again.

A friend said, "Hannah would not want to be the cause of your suffering." I knew that. As a mom, I was grateful that I was the one left to suffer and grieve, not Hannah. If I'd been the one taken first, she might have been in this dark place. Still, I felt cheated by her illness and death. All I could do was tell myself, *This feeling will pass.*

Bill and I with newborn Penelope

29

Signs of Life

In the spring of 2012, the light slowly seeped back into my being. Someone or something was turning my attention away from my dark thoughts. I started to appreciate new beginnings, new accomplishments, and new signs. I witnessed Andrew undergoing his own transformation. Our new house was nearing completion, and I had found a way to participate in some of its final designs. And more mystical and natural signs were appearing to let me know Hannah was still around. I began to believe that I would survive her death.

It had been nearly two years since Hannah visited Isabel to express her concerns for Andrew. Bill and I had been trying to get him help to overcome his depression and obesity—gym memberships, counseling, hypnotherapy—but to no avail. One day, before the start of his senior year of high school, he took it upon himself to get well through disciplined dieting and exercise. By graduation Andrew was a different person. Not only had he lost over 150 pounds, he was now happier, more social, and more engaged with us.

It was an indescribable joy to watch Andrew make these changes in his life. We hadn't been able to prod, convince, or bribe him into changing his ways until he made up his own mind to get healthy. He did it without the help of a trainer or a therapist. But I believed that guardian Hannah had been whispering in his ear.

I was also making more of an effort to take care of myself. In addition to my daily walks, I began getting regular massages from Lily, who had cared so gently for Hannah. I once brought her a glassybaby votive in

Hannah's favorite color, blue, left over from our fundraiser. I couldn't think of a more deserving recipient. When Lily opened her gift, she put her head down and cried. She told me that earlier in the week she had heard Hannah say, "I want to give you a glassybaby in the color of my fingernail polish." Of course, I didn't know that's what Hannah wanted to do, so to me it was a sign that she was still present and still giving. I also felt she was acknowledging my efforts to be good to myself.

Music was becoming more healing than painful for me. Instead of hearing a song like "Firework" and getting sad, I was listening with a different perspective. One day when I was driving home, a song came on the radio that I'd never heard before—Jem's "You Will Make It." When I listened to the words, I heard Hannah singing the song to me, reassuring me that I would survive. The song closes with a slight variation of Mary Elizabeth Frye's famous poem, "Do Not Stand at My Grave and Weep," a favorite of mine:

> Do not stand at my grave and weep,
> I am not there, I do not sleep.
> I am a thousand winds that blow,
> I am the diamond glints on snow,
> I am the sun on ripened grain,
> I am the gentle autumn rain.
> When you awaken in the morning's hush
> I am the swift uplifting rush
> Of quiet birds in circled flight.
> I am the soft stars that shine at night.
> Do not stand at my grave and cry,
> I am not there; I did not die.

Other positive things were happening. The new house was gorgeous. All of our time and effort—largely Bill's—had paid off. From my dream kitchen to the views from every room to the long outdoor deck overlooking the water, I felt very fortunate to be able to call it home. We were so anxious to move in that we lived in its garage apartment for a month while the rest of the house was completed. That August, the four of us, plus two dogs and two cats, were cozy in that one-bedroom space.

We took a vacation for one week of that monthlong wait. Sunriver, Oregon, had been a nearly annual vacation destination for our family from the time the kids were toddlers. Unlike my hesitant return to Maui, this trip to our high-desert vacation home felt like a real holiday. We had a blast, in part due to Andrew's improved energy and fitness level. We played tennis, biked, swam, and worked out at the gym. It was great to take a vacation without worrying about someone. I could barely remember the last time that had been the case. I also had time alone, walking or biking or watching the Mariners' Felix Hernandez pitch a perfect game while Bill and the boys were off mountain biking to a nearby waterfall.

Bill used to take Ryan and Andrew on vacation during spring break, often to the Mariners' spring training. While they had their guy time, Hannah and I had our own getaways. Probably my favorite was at the Seattle downtown Sheraton, where we could order room service, watch pay-per-view movies, swim in the penthouse pool, shop in the city, and visit the aquarium. With Hannah gone, I had been leery of time alone at home while Bill went away with the boys. Their excursion in Sunriver proved that I wouldn't feel left out; in fact, I could enjoy my time alone.

Back home, soon after we moved into our new house, it was time for Andrew to go to college. Much like when Ryan went off to school, Andrew's move into the dorm was a happy occasion. I was thrilled that he was starting this new chapter of his life in a stronger place. Our whole family was looking forward to turning this page.

One evening, shortly after Andrew had left for college, Bill and I were watching a Mariners game on TV when he received a cell phone call from "Unknown." At first, no one responded after he said hello. Bill had a strong feeling that Hannah might be on the other end of the line. He said, "Hannah! Is that you?" He lost the connection and hung up. Then his phone rang again. "Hannah! Is that you?," he said louder. He walked outside to make sure he had good reception. I chuckled to myself, *How far is he trying to reach? Heaven?*

This time there was a response on his phone. "Who do you think it is?" a female voice said. Bill told me it was the kind of thing that Hannah would say and in her same sassy tone. Bill repeatedly asked if it was Hannah. This second call lasted longer than the first, but mostly it was Bill alternating between asking if it was Hannah and saying, "It sounds like you." Bill never got confirmation of who was on the other end of the line. (He regretted not putting the call on speaker so I could hear the voice.) He ended the call but continued to wait and hope that Hannah would call again.

George Anderson and James Van Praagh have said that souls can communicate through electronic devices, such as phones. Bill and I wondered for a long time after the call if Hannah was reaching out to say hello. We never knew for sure, but we believed it was her and took comfort that she had found a way to connect.

Earlier in the summer, I'd received another surprise phone call. The middle school counselor and friend of mine, Patti, called to inform me that she had a letter for us from Hannah. I had no idea that our daughter had written something just before she left school. I learned it was a tradition that the sixth graders write a letter to themselves, which is then given to them as they finish eighth grade. I was excited: more words from Hannah! I was a bit concerned about how the letter would read, since she'd written it when she was declining physically and cognitively. But I was happy to discover it was surprisingly clear and very much in Hannah's voice. Her words were a priceless gift:

> Dear future me,
>
> I'm in sixth grade and when you open this I'll be in eighth grade. I'm going through a cancer treatment. It's called Accutane and Saha. It's making my skin dry. There are two ½ days left of school not including today. It's so exciting!!

When I open my letter in 8th grade I'm going to high school!!!!

<u>YOU</u> deserve it! You've worked so hard in the past years, school, cancer and friends!

You've gone through so so much. It's my brother's birthday today, he turns 18 today, Andrew turned 16, and Adam is almost 30 with a wife named Alexis. I hope they have a baby in the next couple of years. I wonder if my favorite color was still blue and I was wondering what the gas price is in 2 years! Right now it's $3.05. The economy is pretty bad...hoping it will recover soon.

So just keep truckin on! I hope all the cancer has been gone for years and it never comes back ever again!

P.S. My friends are Amanda, Lindsay, Shania, Courtney and Jade. I wanna see if they're my friends still in 8th grade. I hope!

Keep hangin on if my cancer is not gone.

I love ya! See you in 8th grade

Feeling newly inspired, I began looking for signs of Hannah again in nature. One day, Isabel told me a story about crows. She believed they were spiritual messengers. She told me about a time, a few years before Hannah passed, when she was with her sister, who was dying of brain cancer. Isabel and her sister were looking out a large picture window at a field of crows. Suddenly, in Isabel's vision, the crows turned into people. She saw them as folks waiting to greet her sister when she passed. It wasn't until I heard Isabel's story and her belief about crows that I recalled the many crows that had been present outside Hannah's bedroom window at the end of her life, perhaps spirits waiting to greet her.

Eagles had also taken on significance for me. We often see these large, majestic birds in the Puget Sound area, including over the bay where we now lived. My friend Teri had reinforced for me what a blessing they were: she said they were symbolic of her son who had died. In the midst of my cold, dark winter, I had started watching eagles via nest webcams. Not having much energy to be productive, I'd spent hours on the couch watching families of eagles. I was captivated by this close-up view into their lives. I felt uplifted by the success of fledged eaglets but then saddened at the cruelty of a small eaglet dying.

Somehow I felt a kinship with these birds, witnessing their triumphs and tragedies, not to mention their patience and steadfastness in caring for their fragile young. After my hard winter passed, I paid more attention to the adult and juvenile eagles in our neighborhood. Occasionally, I spotted one flying close to our new house. To me, it was a swift hello from my daughter.

Birds had had significance for me even before Hannah was born. Ever since my mom died, I had paid attention to robins. When Claude had called me to tell me Mom had passed, I was standing by my kitchen window at home watching a robin in the early morning grass. In March 2012, when I was beginning to wake from my nightmare winter, I saw robins everywhere. This symbol of spring and new life was another signal to me from Hannah to keep the faith and look forward.

In another bird-related event, Hannah's school wanted to create an outdoor structure in her memory. When they asked our family what we would like it to be, the only thing I could think of was something having to do with birds. Hannah's last meaningful project in school, just when she relapsed, was a bird-mapping assignment to draw birds in our area and write information about them. In the end, the same crew that rebuilt our house constructed a bird-watching platform at her school. I loved that the platform was not only for observing birds, but also a place for friends to gather and talk, just as Hannah would have done with her friends.

The platform was dedicated the weekend of Andrew's high school graduation, when Adam and Alexis were in town. In one week we had had his prom, graduation, and a family reunion. More things had become joyful rather than sad. The new house, the new Andrew, and the new signs all gave me reasons to be hopeful that I could find my way without Hannah by my side.

Ryan, Bill, and Andrew biking
at Sunriver, Oregon

The plaque at Hannah's bird-watching platform

30

Caregiving

With Andrew away at college, my nest was truly empty. At least I wasn't saddled with the grim outlook I'd had the previous year. But I still needed to find something meaningful to do with my time. In addition to looking for signs from Hannah, I needed to listen to my own voice.

One day, while I was out walking the dogs in the woods as I did every morning, a voice inside me began to speak. I heard it say, *Call Robin. Volunteer.* My bereaved friend was coordinating our local Island Volunteer Caregivers (IVC) program, which offers assistance to seniors who are living independently. With my educational background in occupational therapy, not to mention the years of helping my disabled daughter, I knew I could be of service. And some part of me knew that helping others would get me out of my better-but-still-depressed head.

I started by driving seniors around the island for appointments or grocery shopping. Then I became a primary caregiver to a woman who needed a fair amount of help. I finally felt I was doing something worthwhile again. I know that she depended on me and looked to me as more than a volunteer. But it wasn't until I began to help out another woman that I crossed the boundary from volunteer to close friend.

Rae was familiar to me from Grace Church, but I didn't really know her in the beginning. This ninety-four-year-old woman with white hair was tall and strong of build, as I am. Rae was sharp as a tack, opinionated, funny, and a captivating storyteller. She spoke slowly and deliberately, and always amazed me with her keen memory. Rae gave the best

hugs and had the warmest smile. And while she was fiercely independent, she had learned to "put her pride in her pocket," as she said, and
ask for help when she needed it. I learned a lot from her.

Rae had grown up on a Montana ranch during the Depression.
She and her cowboy husband raised their kids there. Then, when she
became a widow over twenty years before I met her, she moved into a
senior apartment to be near her daughter, Jerilyn.

At first Rae and I were pleasant and cordial with each other, but
that's as far as it went. As we spent more time together, we developed
a genuine, mutual fondness. Our grocery shopping trips turned into
three-hour affairs, as we took most of the time to sit down and talk over
biscotti and almond lattes. I found Rae so easy to talk to. She had an
openness and a curiosity about her that belied her age. She drew me
in and soon had me spilling my heart and my guts out to her. She was
warm and caring, but it was her willingness to hear hard things that
made her special. Eventually, she started introducing me as her third
daughter, which I loved. Rae was the mother I didn't have but longed
for; the one with whom I could cry, laugh, and be completely honest.

The thing that bonded us the most was the fact that we were both
bereaved moms. My dear friend had lost her only son, Daniel, in the
Vietnam War. Even though Dan had been gone for nearly fifty years,
tears came to Rae's eyes whenever she talked about him. She shared
tales of Dan's adventures growing up on their ranch, and I told her stories about Hannah. It didn't matter that there was a thirty-nine-year
age difference between us; our hearts were deeply connected. This
wise woman became my counselor, my mentor, my Al-Anon sponsor,
and my friend. I helped her with the practicalities of daily life, but she
gave me so much more than I gave to her. Our common grief of losing
our youngest children permanently cemented our connection, one
bereaved mother to another.

I wish I'd had more time with Rae. Given her choice, she would have
lived longer, but her body gave out on her. She died just days after her
ninety-seventh birthday. I was privileged and honored to be there with

her at home, alongside her family, when she passed. Witnessing her last breath was a blessing. Rae's death at the fine old age of nearly a century made a stark contrast to the death of my young daughter.

When I think back to that voice in my head, urging me to call Robin to volunteer, I believe it was Hannah nudging me into the arms of one of the wisest, most loving women I have ever known. Rae was a model for me on how to do grief, not to mention old age, well. She kept in regular contact with me even when we didn't have something practical to do together. When she sat with me, she was present, focused, and sharp. She liked to listen to my stories as much as tell her own. Rae could access and express her emotions about her loss freely, thereby giving me permission to do the same. And she offered me unconditional love and support, no matter how I was doing on a given day. She often told me that she loved me and that she prayed for me.

In the process of getting to know Rae, I also came to know her youngest daughter. As a tribute to her fallen brother, Jerilyn, along with her mom and her husband, Danaan Parry, had founded PeaceTrees Vietnam in 1995. This organization works to clear landmines and return the land to safe and productive use, and also to build bridges of friendship and understanding between the two former enemies. Rae began working for PeaceTrees by writing thank-you notes to donors. She was a reluctant participant at first, due to her complicated feelings about the country where her son had died. But before long she was saying, "Getting involved with PeaceTrees changed my life."

Rae had discovered that her pain was lessened by connecting to other mothers from both the United States and Vietnam who had lost children in the war. Just as I had found healing in connecting with other bereaved mothers, Rae built friendships with grieving moms and did meaningful work as a means to heal her broken heart.

Volunteering to help seniors maintain their independent living situations was smaller in scope than the work of PeaceTrees, but I knew I was making a difference. I was also receiving something in return. From these bereaved mothers and widows I received a master class in how to go on without Hannah in my life. My work would be different, but had to be meaningful to me.

In the years ahead, I continued looking for ways to be of service. I tried to keep listening to my inner voice and to Hannah's nudges. And I trusted that she would be with me to help.

Rae and I

Jerilyn and I at the PeaceTrees
luncheon, 2019

31

A Sacred Reading

I knew before Hannah died that I would one day get a reading from Steven Forrest on her astrological chart. I had also begun to find writing to be a cathartic and creative source of meaning for me. I even envisioned writing a book that would be a tribute to my daughter. If I was going to write a book about Hannah's soul and the purpose of her life, however, I had to include an astrological perspective. That meant going to the source: my beloved astrology teacher, who had opened my eyes and made my heart sing. Together, Steve and I had pondered Hannah archetypally as a saint or a healer. I wanted to know more clearly why my daughter was born and why she had to die so young. I had done my amateur best to study Hannah's birth chart, separately and up against my own. But I needed a professional reading from a master.

Three years after Hannah died, Bill and I traveled to Steve's home in the Southern California desert to receive his reading of Hannah's chart in person. I didn't have huge expectations, but I knew he would offer us real wisdom, truth, and comfort. I naively thought that I had uncovered pretty much everything about Hannah's natal chart, but after meeting with Steve I realized that what I knew was incomplete. I had been contemplating Hannah's soul as having a more saintly "Mother Teresa" karma, but Steve unearthed deeper, darker elements in her story. After hearing Steve's thoughts, I could understand why these possible dark scenarios hadn't occurred to me. I came away with not only greater insight into her soul, but also some possible answers as to why she had been born into this lifetime and into our family.

When we arrived in the desert, Bill and I stayed at an inn near Steve's home. I had a hard time sleeping the night before the reading; I couldn't wait to hear what he had to say. But I wasn't as nervous and excited as I'd been before meeting with George Anderson, mostly because I knew the astrological terrain and wasn't expecting Hannah to show up.

Steve greeted us like old friends and escorted us into his small home office. I was instantly comfortable; Bill was a bit nervous because he had not met Steve and had a minimal grasp of the astrological language. Steve, an old hippie, looks like a cross between Gandalf and Dumbledore, with the mind of Einstein and the heart of Gandhi. When I first met him at his apprenticeship program in the spring of 2003, I was captivated by his brilliant mind. As he interpreted charts and fielded questions from his students, I couldn't write fast enough to record everything he said. This masterful storyteller, who could hold my attention for hours, used this talent in the art of interpreting a chart.

Steve opened Hannah's reading by speaking philosophically about the mysteries of life and death, particularly when a child dies at a young age. He said, "With death, young or old, we begin to ask, Why were we here in the first place? When you look at a newborn baby, you look in her eyes and there's something ancient, already human in her eyes. You make the assumption that Hannah's soul previously existed in other bodies, other circumstances. She came into this world fully human; kind of a nice one as humans go, and kind of a tragic one in terms of the karmic story."

Steve teaches that the purpose of reincarnation is the evolution of consciousness, with each lifetime offering a period of growth and learning. In previous, less-evolved lives, either we made mistakes that damaged us and yielded consequences in our present lives, or we got some things right but were hurt in the process. Healing these wounds is the evolutionary work of our lives. Evolutionary astrology presumes the karma has "ripened" and a person is now ready to deal with their soul wounds. Steve also presumes that the work may not be from a single past life, but rather from an accumulation of lives resulting in maladaptive behaviors or issues carried over through the emotional memories of the soul.

Steve bypassed his usual descriptive reading of a natal chart and went right to Hannah's karmic story, which he believes gives the reason for why a person is born and why they have the birth chart that they have. He described her soul as coming from a sensitive, vulnerable place, where she was subservient to those around her, either a spouse, a family, or a religious order. Given the planetary signatures, Steve suggested that in a previous life Hannah may have been a victim of abuse, such as that from a shaming, dysfunctional, or possibly violent family. In response, Hannah withdrew or escaped into a spiritual life, a fantasy life, or a dissociated mind. But she was also wired to love those people who may not have been good to her; therefore she obeyed and stayed stuck in a toxic situation. She may have also perpetuated this scenario by falling into a dysfunctional marriage or family system. Given the chart symbolism, Steve even ventured to say that Hannah may have been the victim of sexual abuse, so horrific that it may have cost her her life.

In order to heal the damage to her soul, Hannah needed to be born into a healthy, functional family, based on trust and honesty. Steve said, "Hannah needed a family experience where people were dealing with extremely raw material really honestly. When Hannah attracted death to herself, the reality of her disease compelled a level of intensity, honesty, and directness between you. I think of the three of you together, facing the reality of Hannah's disease, as the epitome of a functional family under an extreme, nightmare experience. I can't look at this chart and say that she would pass at an early age. But she needed to know that family didn't have to be insane, and that she could count on you when times got hard."

Steve spoke of previous lifetimes when Hannah may have obeyed the orders and accepted the secrets and lies of a dysfunctional family. But in this life, Hannah came into the world as a child who needed to be told the truth. Steve said that if we hadn't spoken the truth to her, she would have smelled it. If we had tried to protect Hannah from the truth, we would have hurt her. These statements were difficult to hear, as Bill and I had struggled with the fact that we hadn't spoken directly with Hannah about her impending death. In all other aspects of her life we had been open and honest with her. But in trying to keep some hope alive, we had not dealt openly with the fact that her cancer would kill her.

Hannah's chart also spoke to the need for her to find her voice in this lifetime. Steve said, "In prior lives, she was carrying the internal message of 'you don't have a right to exist, to be seen, or to be heard.'" Given that she had taken a back seat to people close to her in previous lives and did as she was told, Steve said, "Hannah was learning to speak up for herself and take up some space in this life, learning that her needs were just as important or more so than others." He offered the theory that when Hannah became ill, she became the center of things and family revolved around her. Hannah then knew she was loved, and her soul was healed.

Hannah's chart indicated that she came into this life carrying the archetype of the mystic, which often deals with nonmaterial, spiritual work. Steve said, "In this lifetime, Hannah signed a soul contract with God to do the hard work of nonattachment. She had been learning about nonattachment as she got sick. . . . Hannah knew she was dying, and had to deal with the loss of her body. She was also losing the attachment to her karmic narrative of pain that told her to escape, to not trust in family, and to not be truthful with others. She could not have done it without a healthy family dealing honestly with raw stuff and loving her through it."

Steve then brought my chart into the discussion, including why I had given birth to my daughter and what was happening when I lost her. I'd been following the symbolism, but he offered clarity to our collective stories that I couldn't grasp alone. He began by talking about my own karmic story with my ingrained need to be in control, to be responsible for others, and to go above and beyond the call of duty. Steve said,

"What is the effect upon the soul of denying the needs of the heart, the body, and the inner child? The karmic distortion in you, Reba, looks like you were in a position of authority, subjected to high levels of stress and responsibility, and you probably rose to it, you got it right, and it damaged you."

Steve said the remedy for such soul damage is this: "You have an evolutionary need to soften, to feel, to cry with someone with whom you care, someone you consider 'family.' Marriage is also good for you if you find a guy who loves you and is committed to you. This is the therapy in this lifetime."

At the time of Hannah's death, my own chart reflected a period of great pain and transformation. Steve said, "Circumstances were constellating that would soften you, open your heart. What would break the stranglehold of your ability to survive anything? I feel mean saying this, but let's say there's a convention of angels that planned your incarnation. And they said, 'This woman has got to cry. Can we come up with something that would make her cry?' Forgive me."

My karmic story involved being burdened by duties and responsibilities with the underlying feeling of *I can handle anything. Nothing can break me. They'll never see me cry.* Steve said, "You needed to be broken. Let me speculate that losing Hannah was more than you could handle. But you're still here. How come you're still here? How'd you get through that? With a little help from your friends."

Steve went on to affirm the gift of my marriage to Bill. He said, "Here's a classic scenario: a couple loses a child; then three years later, they're divorced. Here, you're still married. I'm glad of that. If you had responded in the karmic way, you would have gone into a period of radical self-sufficiency, gone inside a stone castle with the drawbridge up, and nobody would have seen what was going on inside you. Karma would have come close to driving Bill away from you. It appears that you haven't driven him away, and that's beautiful. Your cutting-edge soul work is about maintaining loving relationships in a spirit of vulnerability."

I also knew from studying Bill's chart that our karmic stories were intertwined; we were each part of the other's evolutionary path. Hannah's death was difficult and painful for us, but also something we were meant to share. Now Bill and I were coming to understand its meaning. Having our daughter opened Bill's heart, while it opened me up to the essential gifts of friendship and family. Together as a family, Bill and I had given Hannah a loving container in which to heal herself.

As an astrologer, I knew that the planets constellating over my chart during Hannah's illness and death were once-in-a-lifetime events. Hannah's life and death not only affected our marriage but also profoundly changed me—in ways I was still learning about.

One of the astonishing aspects of astrology is that when there is a significant, profound, or traumatic event in a life, a cosmic signature of that event is usually present in the chart. Hannah's chart at the time of her death reflected the completion of her work of nonattachment, of letting go of her painful karmic narrative. For Bill and me, Hannah's death was symbolized by traveling planets hitting sensitive parts of our charts, our souls. Coping with Hannah's illness and death was no easy task. But it was part of our souls' journeys.

There was also great truth and great love in the journey with Hannah. I knew in my heart at Hannah's birth that she would help to heal our family in some way, but I could not have foreseen that she was on her own deep healing journey. I believe that we signed a soul contract with Hannah before she was born to love her deeply and to walk beside her as she let go of her earthly life and her karmic pain. Thanks to Steve, we now had a better understanding of the reason Hannah was born into our lives.

Astrology is an ancient, sacred language. My younger self, even at thirty years old, would never have believed that I would subscribe to this art in the latter part of my life. When I began studying astrology in 2002, I had no idea how it would shape my life or my view of the afterlife. When my close girlfriends convinced my skeptical self to sign up for a beginning astrology class, I came to find out that I had a mind for astrology, and I started to believe it was part of what I was born to do. And it answered big questions for me: *Why was I born? What is the purpose of my life?*

Prior to the class, I'd had no idea what astrology was really all about beyond the daily horoscope in the newspaper. I had no idea that it was an ancient art, studied by the great philosophers and scientists of history. Beyond the generic and simplistic nature of "sun sign" astrology, evolutionary astrology—a branch of Western astrology—is a complex, in-depth study of an individual's unique birth chart. Based on thousands of years of observation of the heavens and their correlations with earthly events, the practice requires years of study along with an engaged heart to decipher via the birth chart what a soul is seeking in this lifetime.

Astrology can be a rich source of self-awareness and life purpose. When Hannah lay dying and we had begun separating from each other, I found solace by focusing on her being a soul with a life mission and not just my daughter. Uncovering what her life had been about gave me great comfort, since it's not typical for a mother to outlive a daughter. I felt a deep sense of peace when I began to understand that Hannah's soul had a reason for being that was vaster than I could envision. Her soul was part of something greater, and as much as I loved her, I couldn't stop the inevitable—that her soul's job in this lifetime was finished. Astrology gave me a language to understand that job and that purpose.

I was grateful for Steve's analysis. When Bill and I left his home that sunny day in December, we felt uplifted and joyful, much as we had after seeing George. The contact with Hannah had been less direct but no less meaningful. Hearing about the difficult path her soul had been on and the courage she'd displayed in choosing to go through such an excruciating illness with people who loved her unconditionally was comforting. It wouldn't bring our daughter back, but it clarified her purpose for being. I wasn't sure where I would go next on this journey without Hannah's physical presence, but this reading had been just the medicine I needed. Everyone has a purpose. Now, what would be mine?

Bill and I with Steve Forrest at his home after the
reading, 2013

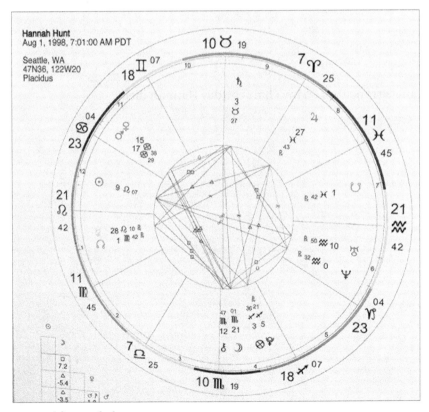

Hannah's natal chart

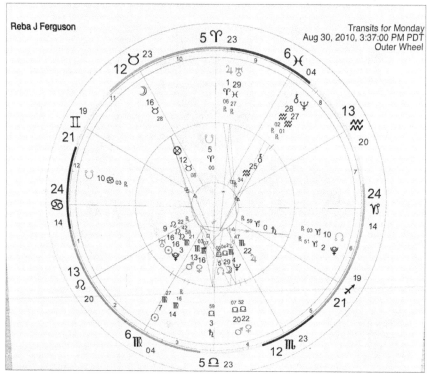

Planets transiting on my chart the day Hannah died

32

Star Map

Hearing from Steve about Hannah's soul purpose offered some closure about her life, but it left me wondering what the purpose of my life would be in the days ahead. I knew I'm here in part to let go of my extreme sense of duty and responsibility and to let others share the burdens and the hard work with me. I need to work on being less in my head and more in my heart, less about the job at hand and more about the process, less about the work and more about my feelings. I need to find, sometimes with others' help, ways to find balance and calm down. Especially in light of losing Hannah, I needed to recover my sense of peace. I turned to the stars to light my way forward.

I knew from previous astrological readings and studying my chart that one way I could find peace was through the creative arts. My birth chart suggested that writing could be one of those paths. During Hannah's illness, I'd found comfort in recording what was happening to her and how I was feeling through journaling and CaringBridge posts. Now I wondered if I could take it a step further. *Will I be able to find the courage to say what is important to me and what is meaningful and helpful to other people? Can I make peace with Hannah's death by sharing her story?*

In the first year after Hannah died, most of my writing took place privately, in my journal, but I occasionally shared how I was doing on CaringBridge. My bereaved friends and I began to write and share in our small group, which we called the Shitty First Draft Writing Group, a nod to Anne Lamott. It felt safe to put myself out there with these women, even if some days there was little writing and more talking.

Writing about my feelings and experiences seemed to be a good way to handle my fluctuating grief. The group gave me the courage to take my first steps in writing Hannah's story.

I read over my journals and CaringBridge posts in preparation for telling her story in a book. But reliving what we'd been through only made me sadder and more depressed. It was too soon, too painful, and too close to my heart. I had to put the work aside.

A couple months later, during one of our writing group meetings, hardly anyone had done the homework of responding to a prompt so we simply shared our ideas for creative projects. Teri spoke about wanting to write a children's book, as a tribute to her son, from the viewpoint of an eagle. Her mention of a kids' book sparked a creative idea in my mind.

What if I were to tell Hannah's story through the lens of her birth chart? I could use symbolism from nature to depict the parts of her astrological chart, parts of herself, in a way that would be beautiful and accessible to all ages.

The creative wheels started turning. The text would be short and simple and lyrical. I would use images from nature that correspond to astrological representations to describe Hannah. A lion or a sunflower might represent her Leo sun. An orca whale, swimming in its family pod, would show her Scorpio moon. Her Cancer Venus would be depicted as a mother bird with a nest of babies, representing her many friends. One page would offer the astronomical facts of the planet and the star constellation, while the facing page would show the astrological interpretation. I would share Hannah's story in an artistic and informative way, presenting all of the wonderful pieces of my healthy daughter without focusing on her illness or death. This book felt easier to write than the emotional and heavy story I had originally envisioned.

My niece, Annie, was an artist; perhaps she would be interested in doing the illustrations. I would access my artistic sensibilities to create the design and text of each page, in conjunction with Annie's artwork. The book would also serve as an educational resource for readers to learn something about astrology beyond the simplistic sun signs they knew from their newspaper horoscope. The more I thought about it, the more I got excited. For the first time in a while I had something productive and creative to do that also seemed like fun.

Right away, Annie was on board, and we made a good team. She understood my concept and could visualize the art. I would give her the basic required elements of each illustration, and she could create the planets, the constellations, and the astrological scenes. But it was a lot of work for her. On top of her regular job, the number of illustrations I was asking for required a significant time commitment on her part. And, in an effort to simplify and clarify the book, I periodically updated my requests, changing what each page should look like. As it turned out, writing and giving illustration notes for this "Star Map" book was a lot more difficult than I'd originally envisioned.

I needed help with writing and clarifying what Hannah's book would depict, and the universe delivered. I'd been working alone and had had little critique or assistance with the writing other than from Annie and my first astrology teacher, Andrea. As fate—or Hannah—would have it, I turned on my computer one day to see a Facebook post from Jennifer Louden announcing that she had an opening in one of her writing retreats.

Jen is a writer, friend, and former islander. I took the plunge, signed up, and a month later found myself on an idyllic farm in rural Vermont with a group of other women writers. At first I felt totally out of my league. I had no formal training in memoir or creative writing. I only had my journal posts and a smattering of folks who'd said I should write a book. Despite my doubts, I immersed myself in the writing and the company in this safe, loving, contained space. I received instruction, creative prompts, and feedback from not only Jen but also the other women on the retreat.

I returned to Jen's retreat at the same farm the following year. I was getting clarity on how to structure and simplify *Hannah's Star Map*— and just beginning to write a chapter for this book. I've since taken a couple of Jen's online workshops, especially when I needed to get back into the writing habit. I credit Jen with giving me the tools that help me to believe I can be a writer. Besides my literary friends, my editors, including Nancy Silk and Beth Wright, helped me hone my writing skills. I have learned to ask for and accept help, just as my birth chart suggested I should. Leaning in to the support of other writers and editors has helped further my writing craft.

Working on *Hannah's Star Map* also gave me the time and the clarity to eventually return to the "Big Book" about her, the one you are holding in your hands. With time and healing, I reached a better place from which to revisit the scenes of Hannah's cancer journey and what has transpired since her death.

As the years have passed and my heart feels less broken, I'm also turning to other creative activities that fuel my Leo self. Handcrafts such as quilting, sewing, and cross-stitching had always been favorite pastimes of mine, mostly arts I picked up from my fellow crafty Leo mom. For a long time I didn't have the energy, the heart, or the courage to initiate and follow through with any art project. Five years after Hannah died, I pulled her favorite clothes out of a bin in our basement to make a memorial quilt. I'd wanted to make it for years, but I hadn't had the heart to cut up her favorite shirts, even if I would be making something meaningful. At last I was finally ready to turn the items Hannah used to wear into something that I could wrap myself up in when I was cold or especially missing her. Creating the quilt was another sign to me that I was further down the road in my grief.

Feeling less devastated by Hannah's death, I've been better able to focus on my life's purpose. And, just as my chart suggested, I have needed others' support to accomplish this work. *Hannah's Star Map* gives me an opportunity to creatively show my whole daughter—her personality, her values, her mind, and her heart—in all the qualities she took with her after she passed onto another realm, according to George Anderson. I've needed Annie's help to create the illustrated book. And, in tackling this memoir with the help of my friends and other writers and editors, I've found the courage to revisit the joy of having Hannah and the pain of losing her. Both books are a tribute to Hannah, her perfect, infinite self. In reflecting on Hannah's soul, the purpose of her life, and her ongoing presence, I am finding my new path.

With Jen Louden at the Vermont
retreat, 2016

Annie's astrological
illustration of Hannah's moon
in Scorpio

Annie's astronomical illustration of
the moon and Scorpius constellation

Hannah's quilt

33

The Tea Party

Turning my darkest loss into hopeful light for others became my other mission.

In the fall of 2014, Ryan and I attended a family open house at Dr. Olson's lab at the Fred Hutchinson Cancer Research Center. Late in the afternoon, as the sun was setting on this rooftop gathering, Jim played a recorded song that paid tribute to children who had died of brain cancer, including Hannah. By the end of the song, Ryan and I had wrapped our arms around each other as tears streamed down our faces. Before we left the Hutch that night, Jim asked me if I would be interested in holding another Hannah's Hopeful Hearts event to support his lab, as we had done in 2010. I couldn't say no to Jim or to the opportunity to fundraise for a cure. But this time, I wouldn't have Hannah by my side.

It had been over four years since Hannah died, so I thought I could handle another fundraiser, but I didn't realize what I was getting myself into. My planning self kicked in, and the event quickly formulated in my mind. It would be held again at Grace Church. Besides Jim, I also wanted to include Dr. Mike Jensen, a fellow islander, to support his immunotherapy research for pediatric cancer at Seattle Children's. Jim and Mike would present their current work, followed by some entertainment. I had just discovered St. Paul de Vence, a great indie-folk band, when I attended their concert at Grace. Fortuitously, they were also part of a musical compilation CD that was raising funds for Dr. Olson's work.

Rather than the elaborate buffet we'd had in 2010, I put out a call for dessert cupcakes, one of Hannah's favorite treats. I would ask Jeanette to prepare an array of appetizers, assisted by some of Hannah's friends. And we would hire a professional auctioneer to raise the money. No silent auction, no big feast, just wine, cupcakes, light snacks, great music, and a call for donations. Still, it became quite a time-, labor-, and heart-intensive project for me.

At our 2010 fundraiser, Hannah was still alive and I'd held a sliver of hope that some of the money raised might actually save her life. Now, in spring 2015, I was trying to survive without my daughter while putting on a benefit in her memory. I had decided that I would briefly tell Hannah's story that evening, even though the thought of standing in front of hundreds of guests made me feel incredibly anxious. I am not a public speaker. My voice is often shaky, even talking in front of a small group. In order to tell Hannah's story, what she endured, and what she meant to me in front of hundreds of people, I needed some help.

About six weeks before the event, I was in an island store when I overheard a customer talking about a local medium she had visited. Bill and I had been uplifted by our time with George Anderson, so I was instantly intrigued. I got the medium's phone number, contacted her, and met her the next day.

I had no idea what to expect when I arrived at Heather's house. Unlike George, she wasn't well known, hadn't done television or radio shows, and didn't have a résumé of famous clients. But she was warm and loving and invited me in with questions and conversation.

Fairly early in the session, Heather told me she saw a tea party of three young girls. She asked me if I liked to bake cakes or cupcakes and whether I was preparing for a large party, since the girls were making cakes for their own gathering. I acknowledged that I was but didn't give her any more details. Heather described the three girls: one blond, one brunette, and one redhead. She told me the blond had the initials *HH*. At this point I was crying because I could tell she was seeing Hannah. Heather also said she was seeing a teal-blue heart, Hannah's favorite color and, to me, symbolic of her loving spirit. Between the initials, the cupcakes, and the blue heart—not to mention the preparations for an event—I believed that Heather had contacted Hannah.

I later discerned that the brunette girl was likely Katie, Karen's daughter. Since Katie's family supported Dr. Jensen's research, her story would also be told at the fundraiser. Less clear was the redheaded girl, but in my heart I knew it was my redheaded friend Stefanie's daughter, Carey, who had died shortly after her preterm birth. Stefanie was involved in our fundraiser, and her whole family had annually participated in the Run of Hope. Her husband had even done the Seattle-to-Portland bike race in Hannah's memory. I knew that this tea party meant that our girls were working right alongside us, preparing for the big event.

I received another special gift the day I saw Heather. My dad, whom I hadn't seen in nearly thirty years, appeared. When Heather saw my dad, he was standing behind me, saying that he was watching over Andrew. My son had had a tough year, as Hannah had foretold, but he was doing well then. Still, it was heartwarming to hear that Andrew's guardian angel was my dad.

I left Heather's that day feeling bolstered that I could tell Hannah's story at the event because I had gotten clear proof yet again that Hannah's spirit was alive and well, and that she was with me. As I prepped for my speech, the words came quickly. Then, to ease my anxiety, I practiced it over and over out loud on my morning dog walks until I'd memorized it.

On the night of the fundraiser, I was nervous, excited, and ready to talk about my daughter. After Jim introduced me, I stood up in front of the standing-room-only crowd, took a deep breath, and began my talk. Here is an excerpt of what I said:

> You know, Jim didn't really know my daughter, Hannah. I've often said, if I ever write a book it will be titled "This Is NOT My Daughter!!" Jim knew Hannah as a product of her cancer surgery and treatment—an angry, rude, uncooperative, weak, wildly emotional girl. Sassy maybe, but not as kind or as sharp as she once was.

Jim did not know my brave, beautiful, wise-beyond-her-years, funny, athletic, fiercely independent, hopeful girl, who was the light of my life.

I've often thought—what if Jim's Tumor Paint was available when Hannah had brain surgery back in 2007? Maybe the Tumor Paint would have lit up the two hundred or so cells that may have been missed, so the bad cells wouldn't have been left to seed in her brain and become the cancer that would take her life. And maybe the surgeons wouldn't have accidentally taken healthy brain tissue that they couldn't differentiate from cancerous cells, causing her to have to learn to walk, and speak, and dress, and think all over again. . . .

And maybe if one of Project Violet's drug candidates was available to Hannah to treat her cancer instead of the chemotherapy that poisoned her body . . . she may have been spared the hair loss, the feeding tubes, the multiple hospitalizations for secondary infections, the blood transfusions, the lost time with friends and family and school.

And maybe, too, she wouldn't have had to have radiation to her whole brain and spine. Radiation is kryptonite to a growing brain and body. It stopped her growth and diminished her brain capacity in so many ways. Hannah used to pride herself on being an excellent student. That was taken away from her.

And maybe if Mike Jensen's immunotherapy for brain tumors was ready when she relapsed, Hannah would still be here with us. When Hannah's cancer returned in 2009, we turned to Jim Olson, the expert on her particular brain tumor. But six years ago, the only thing Jim could offer us was a hug and a heartfelt "I'm so sorry."

Fast-forward to today, and things look a lot brighter for kids who will be diagnosed with cancer in the future. Hannah would want us to keep fighting and not give up. Hannah would want us to keep supporting these doctors who are finding cures not only for brain cancer, but for all childhood cancers. Even the ones for which there is currently no cure. Just as she wrote about in her sixth-grade essay, Hannah wanted to be part of the cure. I know that Jim and Mike are passionate about finding treatments that kill the cancer without harming the child. Hannah and Katie would want us to keep fighting and not give up.

Karen and I are in that club that no one wants to belong to—the club of mothers who have lost children. No dad wants to go through the hell of watching their child suffer and die. And no brother wants to grow up and live the rest of their lives without their sister. So why do I stand here with my heart in my throat and organize a fundraiser which is basically a memorial to my daughter? Because as Carin Towne, Ben's mom, once said, "If parents like ourselves who understand the ultimate price of childhood cancer don't stand up and say NO MORE, then who will?" Thank you all for standing up with us.

After seeing Heather, I knew that Hannah was standing with me as I spoke these words. She would want me to keep fighting the fight to spare other children the suffering she had endured. I knew that someday there would be miracles for kids like Hannah and Katie. I also knew that Hannah was no longer weak, sick, and in pain, but rather the strong, wise, feisty, and funny girl she was at her core—a girl who enjoyed the company of her friends. From a giggly girls' gathering to a major fundraising event, Hannah showed up for the parties. And I was grateful for that.

By the time the night was over, we had raised over $200,000 for the Olson and Jensen labs. While it was a great success, putting on the event had been a lot more difficult for me than it had been in 2010. Still, hearing from Hannah through Heather had given me the strength and confidence to stand before a packed crowd and tell her story.

At the start of the event, Jim had played the music video of the song that Ryan and I had first heard on his lab's rooftop, OK Sweetheart's "Safe." The video featured pictures of the patients he had lost to cancer, including Hannah. I listened to the sniffles and crying around the room, mostly coming from Hannah's friends. I'd cried too when I first heard the song. But now that I'd heard from Hannah again, it didn't hurt as much. I was more at peace with her just being someplace else.

Safe
They say you're in a better place
Well, I want to come visit you there
And I know we've got to say goodbye
But I'm lonely and I needed a little more time
And I miss you most of all
When the days go by and you're not in them all
And I feel this in my soul
I want to see you safe at home
I want to see you safe at home
They say that time will ease the pain
But they won't even show their faces
And they seem to have a lot to say

But I don't think they know anything at all
Cuz I miss you most of all
When the days go by and you're not in them all
And I feel this in my soul
I want to see you safe at home
I want to see you safe at home
Oh, I will not forget you
How could I forget you?
I will not forget you

I am learning to live without my daughter, some days better than others. I wish she were still at home with me and her family and friends. But thanks to Heather's gifts and Hannah's communication, I know that she's safe and well where she is.

In memory of Katie and Hannah

Dr. Jim Olson and I at the HHH fundraiser

The crowd during the call for donations

34

Her Last Breath

I knew from my own birth chart that helping people through grief was part of my spiritual path. This part of my identity was reflected in a symbol in my chart, the wounded healer. Later, with the help of another astrologer, I discovered new information about Hannah through the astrological "weather" present at the time of her death.

A significant feature in my chart, directly across from my sun, is the planetoid Chiron. This small, asteroid-like body between the orbits of Saturn and Uranus has been known in the astrological world in the past forty-some years as the wounded healer. In Greek mythology, Chiron—kind teacher, musician, and healer—was mortally wounded by a poison arrow, resulting in unbearable pain. But because he was immortal, he couldn't die. He finally gave up his immortality by helping to free Prometheus and was then released to live in the stars with the gods. In astrological counseling, the idea is that we can heal ourselves when we help to heal others.

According to Steve Forrest, our consciousness can be changed and our pain lessened when we focus on another's pain. Conversely, when we wallow in our pain and don't reach out to others in a healing manner, our compassionate gifts are wasted. An example of a wounded healer is a sponsor in Alcoholics Anonymous who has been in recovery for a while and can be a mentor for a more recently recovered member in the program. As Steve says, "Miraculous transformation of our pain may arise as we respond in a healing, mentoring fashion to others' hurts and needs."

After Hannah's death, I initially hated the idea that I would become this type of helping person. I felt mortally wounded and wallowed in my grief. But, years down the road, I became that support for individuals who were more newly grieving. It wasn't until recently that I appreciated Chiron's placement in my birth chart: in the eighth house, which has correlations with death, and directly across from my second house sun. My identity (my sun) was affected by my experiences with a lot of death, especially Hannah's, shaping who I was in the world as a wounded healer.

Just as I was about to write the final chapter of *A Soul Lives On,* I discovered another astrologer who had combined astrology and grief in a memoir. In her book, *Star Sisters,* Linda "Moonrabbit" Zlotnick shares stories of life with her twin sister, grief over her loss, and the astrological signatures that appeared as significant markers during her sister's illness and death. She also describes a new astrological tool that revealed itself to her during this period: the death chart. This revolutionary chart is a picture of the planets at the date, time, and place of a person's death. Moon has been working with the death chart for years and has found it useful not only in revealing the condition of the soul upon the death of the body but also in counseling and supporting those who are grieving.

I felt compelled to contact Moon after I read her book. I wanted her to do a reading of Hannah's death chart. When we first spoke on the phone, Moon was knowledgeable and compassionate, especially in her expression of heartfelt concern over the death of my daughter. She gave me time to talk about the final days and hours of Hannah's life, as she has found listening to a person in grief to be just as vital as dispensing astrological insights. I told her I couldn't imagine losing an identical twin. Together, we acknowledged the agonizing pain, whether it be over the loss of a child or a twin.

Before I read Moon's book, it had never occurred to me to draw up a separate astrological chart for the time of Hannah's passing. I had studied the transiting and progressed planets at the time of her death, as well as her natal chart, alone and with Steve Forrest. I was very curious what new information would be revealed in her death chart.

It included several notable features. The planet Pluto was rising or "dawning" and conjoined to the dwarf planet Ceres. Moon commented that she seldom sees this placement of Pluto, which may be correlated with death, in such a chart. Moon interpreted Ceres as representing me, the mother. (To the Greeks, Ceres was Demeter, who lost her daughter, Persephone, to Pluto in the underworld.) Moon felt that Ceres's proximity to Pluto in this chart symbolized that Hannah knew I was with her at the time of her death. This was touching to me, especially since Hannah had been so uncommunicative in her final weeks.

The North Node of the Moon, the soul intention, was in the sign Capricorn and was also connected to Pluto and Ceres. This symbolism suggested that at the time of her death, Hannah had completed her soul's long and difficult work when she passed. Moon's interpretation echoed what Steve Forrest had said.

Another planetary configuration suggested a conflict or challenge for Hannah in reaching her last breath. I talked with Moon about how Hannah had lingered in her last weeks, repeatedly approaching and then retreating from death's door. For me, this push-pull corresponded to Hannah's reluctance to say goodbye and leave her family and friends in the physical world. Death was calling, but Hannah waited until she could finally, and suddenly, let go of her ties to her loved ones. George Anderson had also commented that he felt Hannah left her body quite quickly.

Moon noted a couple of other features in this unique chart. At the time of Hannah's death, the planets Neptune (related to one's soul) and Chiron (related to a wound) were conjoined. Moon interpreted this to mean that Hannah's wound, her illness, was instrumental to her spiritual path. This idea was compatible with what Steve had said about Hannah drawing the extreme experience of her illness into her body so that she would have her family and close friends to walk with on the intense and intimate journey to her death, releasing her from her karmic narrative of pain and abuse from a toxic family in a previous life.

Moon spoke of a solar eclipse as a significant marker in Hannah's life. Although eclipses are a big part of her professional work, they were relatively unfamiliar to me. As she explained them, eclipses can be signatures or triggers of a new chapter in a life. Moon pointed out that there had been a solar eclipse on July 11, 2010, six weeks before Hannah died. Just a few days prior to the eclipse, Hannah had been airlifted to Children's Hospital. Shortly afterward hospice came on board, ushering in the dying chapter of Hannah's life. In her death chart, this eclipse fell in her eighth house (often associated with death) and on my ascendant (my persona). Moon described the eclipse as the beginning of a new identity for me with the loss of my daughter.

Moon also discussed the planets that were traveling over the planets on my natal chart at the time of Hannah's death. Most of these points were familiar to me, as I had discussed them with Steve. However, Moon saw the signature of Saturn transiting over my North Node of the Moon at the nadir of my chart as representing an ending in my family of origin, possibly a karmic or genetic closure to family dynamics that had gone on for generations. Steve had already addressed Hannah's illness and death, bringing closure and release to her karmic narrative, but perhaps our shared journey had also closed some chapter of my family story, going back to my ancestors.

Hearing Moon speak of an ending to family dynamics that may have existed in my family for generations made me wish my parents were still alive to talk to about what this could mean for all of us. What had they experienced or witnessed as children growing up in their families? Was a cycle being broken in the way in which children were being raised in our families, generation after generation?

Bill and I had worked hard to raise our children differently from how we were brought up. Hannah initiated a new level of truth telling, so once our sons became adults, we tried to have deeper, more honest relationships with them. We tried *not* to avoid the proverbial "elephant in the room," daring to ask the hard questions, listening for our children's points of view, engaging in meaningful conversations, and working to get at their underlying feelings or intentions. I believe every parent strives to do better for their kids than what they experienced. Hannah's death may have ushered in a new way of parenting for us.

Would Hannah's death give birth to a new era of openness and honesty in our families? I had longed for more trust and intimacy with my parents. I've certainly experienced more of that closeness with my own children. Was Hannah's life truly meant to be a larger healing force, not just for her soul but also for her extended family, past, present, and future? Did Hannah's death mean that family members in generations to come could now put genuine truth and pain on the table in the spirit of love and commitment?

I thought I had gleaned as much information as I could about Hannah's soul, including the reason for her birth, through astrological readings, but I was still learning. Now, thanks to Moon and her reading of Hannah's death chart, I had learned more about my daughter's departure from this life. I was comforted to know and believe that at the time of her passing Hannah knew I was near, that she was reluctant to leave her family, that her cancer had been instrumental in her soul's journey, and that she knew when the time was right to leave her body. This information about the condition of Hannah's soul at the time of her death was new to me. I was also coming to appreciate the role in my life as a wounded healer, walking with others through their own grief.

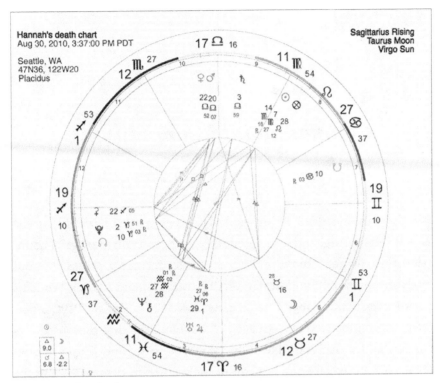

Hannah's death chart

35

Compassionate Companions

In the winter of 2016, Robin invited me to join a local grief group she was facilitating, and I accepted. Having been trained by grief counselor Alan Wolfelt, Robin and her co-leader formed a group of about twelve women, half widows and half bereaved moms. Using Wolfelt's book *Understanding Your Grief,* we met monthly in the local IVC office. Each session focused on sequential "touchstones" that prompted discussion and writing around individual mourning and common grief responses. Between knowing half of the women in the group from the island and having had years to cope with Hannah's death, I was eager to actively do more healing.

Robin tenderly led each session. The evening began with a candle-lighting ceremony in which we each said our beloved's name out loud, followed by a check-in. I was quickly comfortable in these gatherings, having known Robin and Teri from our small bereaved group. I was grateful that we talked about the lifetimes of the ones we missed as much as we talked about their deaths. We shared pictures, mementos, and stories about our loved ones and what they meant to us. I was usually happy to talk about Hannah, but sometimes when I shared about her happy, healthy childhood or her nightmarish illness, I cried. Years earlier I wouldn't have been so brave as to talk about my deepest feelings about her without completely falling apart.

In between sessions we used reading and writing exercises to reflect upon our memories and feelings. Each of us then had opportunities in the group to describe the beloved ones we were missing and talk about what we were currently doing to move forward in our lives.

We each tended to gravitate toward those in the group who had had a similar loss. The widows in our group happened to be relatively new in their grief, whereas the moms had had years to learn to live without their children. The mom group seemed to be in better shape, just by virtue of having had more time with their grief.

A couple of these moms had lost their adult children to a sudden illness or accident. One woman had lost her adult daughter to cancer. No one else in our group had lost a child as young as Hannah. We weren't in a grief competition, but sometimes I reflected on how terrible it was for me to lose a twelve-year-old. Hannah was old enough to have developed a personality and create a life with people she loved. And yet she was far from having accomplished many things that young adults had, such as graduating or living independently or getting married. Hannah's death seemed especially cruel to me.

In the following year, as I grew stronger and better able to cope, another opportunity arose. Robin and two psychologists had begun a grief program on the island called Compassionate Companions. Volunteers were trained and then paired with a member of the community who had recently lost a loved one. The pairing was intended not for therapy but for support and companionship. When Robin asked me if I would like to go through the training, I said yes. It gave me another way to be of meaningful service.

Given that there were more widows than bereaved parents at the time, I was matched with a widow. She had a number of physical disabilities that were exacerbated by her grief and created obstacles to our getting together. We only met a couple of times before she moved off the island, as she never was able to settle into this new place, away from the Midwest home where she had lived with her husband. I tried to dismiss the feeling that I had failed her in some way; I focused on the fact that she wasn't in the right place physically or emotionally to receive support.

My next companion was also a widow, but our match felt Hannah-sent. She reminded me a little of Rae: we could talk easily about anything. She was lonely and sad and seemed to relish my company. I visited her weekly, listening to her tell stories of her life with her husband and reassuring her that her tears were natural. Some days we took walks, did chores, or watched movies.

I knew she would be alone on Thanksgiving, so I came up with an idea to bake her dessert. I made cute mini-pies alongside the pies I was making for my family. When I delivered them in a basket with Häagen-Dazs ice cream, she screamed with delight. I realized driving home that I had taken something that I would have loved doing with Hannah—baking—and turned it into a present for a grieving friend. It no longer hurt to think of what I was missing with my daughter; I had found a way to share it as a gift.

Months after I began seeing this widow, a friend of mine I hadn't seen regularly for years suddenly lost her husband. Without being formally assigned as her companion, I started visiting her, giving her time to talk and cry. We renewed our friendship through sharing our grief.

It feels good to be giving back to these women, instead of sucking the life out of whomever I might be around, as I'd felt when I was newly in the depths of my grief. Some days now, when my life feels difficult, I feel rejuvenated by spending time with these widows. It's not that I'm comparing my less-sad life with theirs. There's a healing, energetic exchange that occurs when two people openly share their broken hearts. The loss of a spouse is obviously different from the loss of a child, but the love can be just as strong.

With the passing of time and work with my grief, I can now be present for those who are new to this road that nobody wants to travel. I can listen to another's deep sadness without it triggering my own. I can hold space for a person who is mourning just by showing up and being present for their needs and feelings. It's a better place than the early days of grief. And it helps to know that I can show someone else who's hurting that it's possible to come out of that darkness.

It's part of why I'm here in this life: to share the pain and make the burdens lighter for others. It's part of why I was born. As Ram Dass, whom Robin is fond of quoting, said, "We're all just walking each other home."

Thanksgiving mini-pies for my care receiver

Being a compassionate companion for Jerilyn at a
family supper after Rae's death

36

My Hopeful Heart

S ome days, just when I think I'm doing fine and able to attend to
others' concerns or my new activities, grief knocks me down again.

This past Thanksgiving, Hannah's seventeen-year-old cat, Leia, died.
We adopted her as a kitten from the local shelter when Hannah was six
years old. Leia's sudden death wasn't unexpected; we knew her time
was running out. A month earlier, she appeared to have a seizure. A couple of trips to the animal clinic didn't provide any definitive answers,
but the vet presumed Leia had some form of brain cancer. I found it a
rather cruel twist of fate that Leia would go out with the same disease
that took Hannah. Mercifully, Leia died quickly, without intervention.
When I found her one morning, still in my chair, I sobbed. My heart was
broken all over again.

I tried to take solace in the fact that Hannah has her again now. But
from the moment I found her to hours later, when we buried Leia in
Hannah's garden, I cried. Even I was surprised by my overwhelming
sadness. Caroline tried to comfort me by reminding me that Hannah
has a whole herd of pets with her now who have been part of our family—dogs Katy and Buddy and cats Jesse, Alex, Jenny, and now Leia.
All of our animals had longer lifespans than Hannah, but now they are
reunited with her. I have to admit to some jealousy.

We have always had cats and dogs, but when our kids were little, we
also had pet rats. Many people hated walking into the room with the
large glass aquarium holding these long-tailed rodents. But they were
very social, easy pets for young children. After many rats came and

went, the last surviving one died of a large tumor. When Hannah witnessed that rat's death, she said, "No more! I don't want to bury another pet."

As I get older, I'll bury more pets and friends and family members, some more difficult than others. I imagine the losses won't get any easier, but maybe my recovery won't be so prolonged as it was for Hannah. I recovered from Leia's death fairly quickly, after a deep dive into mourning her and my daughter all over again.

Sometimes it helps to get a reminder that Hannah's not really gone, just in another dimension. Last year, I found another person who was able to make contact with Hannah. With no luck in receiving clear, verbal messages myself, I discovered another medium, Suzanne Giesemann.

A former naval commander, Suzanne discovered her spiritual abilities after the loss of her stepdaughter and unborn grandson. Following that personal tragedy and the events of 9/11 during her government tenure, Suzanne retired from the military and began a quest to develop her psychic gifts. Her journey began much as mine did—devouring books on the afterlife, including George Anderson's work, noticing signs and synchronicities that couldn't be coincidental, and seeking out credible mediums who could potentially make contact with her daughter.

Eventually, through formal studies, deepening meditation practices, and conducting her own readings, Suzanne sharpened her psychic abilities. But she wasn't content to simply accept thoughts and images that might have come from her own consciousness. As she began to offer readings to others, this former skeptic sought to bring forth evidence— facts she couldn't possibly have known ahead of time—from the soul in the hereafter, such as the cause of death, what the individual had done in their life, or events in the lives of their loved ones still on Earth.

I felt deeply connected to Suzanne as I read her books. Two of them, *Still Right Here* and *Messages of Hope*, are among her growing repertoire of resources available to those in grief or recovery from deep loss. I especially loved finding out that Suzanne's birthday is August 1, the same as Hannah's. Not only that, but Suzanne was born on her mother's birthday, as I was. This fellow Leo sun woman has found a new life, transforming her grief by sharing her intuitive gifts in a generous, creative, and loving way.

Just as I was writing about wanting more of a connection to Hannah, Suzanne provided it to me. I had written to her to express my gratitude for her books and her life's work. She responded immediately, affirming my work on this book and my quest to know that Hannah's spirit continues. I sent Suzanne a picture of Hannah, and she replied, "Oh, Reba, she's so beautiful. I can feel the love. Thank you for sharing your Hannah with me! I don't usually tune in on the spot, but I sense her talking about a necklace you wear all the time in her honor (lots of moms do, but I can't deny this information right now). It feels as if it is a piece of her somehow."

I was thrilled to receive this latest message, and it was spot on. I always wear the silver heart necklace that Alli had given Hannah. I first started wearing it after she died. I needed the physical reminder that she had been my daughter. Now it reminds me that she is always with me. It was comforting to know, once again, that Hannah knows of my current activities, and I have Suzanne to thank for delivering the message. I feel less broken when I'm reminded of Hannah's continued existence.

I don't know if I'll ever be able to directly contact Hannah or my loved ones in the spirit world. I may need to depend on the messages I receive from friends and others who have that gift. But I can rely on faith, given the evidential proof I've received, that while I may not see Hannah, she's still alive in spirit.

Choosing to have Hannah was an act of faith. I had no definitive proof of her existence when I first heard Hannah's soul calling. My own intuition and heart told me that she was looking to be born into our family. No one else needed to tell me that. Without evidence, I know that before we were born Hannah and I signed soul contracts with each other to walk this life together. I gave birth to Hannah, believing that our souls had work to do together. Before she was born, at her bedside as she lay dying, and for years afterward, I have tried to see Hannah's life from a soul perspective.

Knowing in my heart and soul that Hannah was destined to be my daughter is different from living with the deep sadness of her mortal passing. As a human mom, I might not have tried to get pregnant with her if I'd known how her life would end. When I stood at my mom's bedside and told her I was thinking of having another baby thanks to her, I never dreamed that child's life would last only twelve years.

When I fell in love with the girl Hannah was becoming, her brain cancer diagnosis tore at my heart. It seemed preposterous. In the last three years of her life, she endured unfathomable pain and suffering that no parent would ever want to witness. When Hannah's prognosis became terminal, I hated that I would become the bereaved mom—not the proud mom of my graduate daughter, not the mother of the bride, not the grandmother present as her daughter gave birth. I felt robbed, not only of Hannah's unlived future, but of mine.

For a long time before and after she died, I was racked with guilt that I had brought a child into this world for my own selfish purposes. Even after she died, it was heartbreaking to hear Hannah say through George, "If I had to do it all over again, I'd have to think about it. It was a lot to go through." If I'd known the cost ahead of time, my earthly self might never have agreed to our deal.

From a soul's perspective, I hope Hannah got exactly what she needed. I hope she knew she was loved throughout her life, but especially in those last difficult years. I hope she got her opportunities to speak up, share her truth, and ask for what she needed. I hope her soul accomplished what it came here to do. As much as I miss my daughter, I'm grateful that I was able to play a part in her soul's journey. I believe that Hannah's life here was whole and complete. Mine is still a work in progress.

I'm not the same person I was before Hannah died. A part of me died when she left. I've recovered some of my old self, let go of some of the old me, and, in the cauldron of her leaving, transformed what remained into a new version of me. Before her death I was a wife, a mother, a friend, a health care professional, and an aspiring astrologer. On the inside, I was often insecure, uncertain, afraid, skeptical, quiet, and self-sufficient. I was more selfish with what I wanted. I wasn't certain that I'd obtained the correct college degree. I doubted my parenting skills. I questioned the legitimacy of astrology. I feared death.

In the early days after her passing, I felt horribly sad, gutted, and adrift. I felt my life had no purpose. I no longer wanted to live. Slowly, I opened myself to new and deeper friendships. I learned to lean on other women who were also missing their children. I became more discerning with my time and energy, choosing more carefully whose company I kept. I appreciated my husband and my sons more. I opened my eyes to other, more spiritual realms.

As the years have passed, I'm finding purpose and joy again in my life. I'm finding truth and meaning in my astrological practice. I've become a mother bear when it comes to the needs and feelings of my adult children. I'm less timid, more outspoken. I'm more selfless, more giving of my time and talents. I'm less shy about asking for help. I am more grateful for the blessings in my life. I am a believer in eternal life.

Hannah helped me to live into my soul's intentions. Walking with her along the intimate and horrific path to the end of her life opened my eyes to why I am here. Discovering new purposes for my life, I know that I am more than a wife or a mother or a grandmother. I am also a writer, an astrologer, and a grief counselor. None of these are official job titles, but I know they're my life's work. And I now know that there are people in my life to support me and walk with me. I don't have to know it all or do it all alone. I'm not perfect, but I believe I'm a truer version of the person God intended me to be.

❋ ❋ ❋

Hannah's life and death have been healing gifts to me.

If I hadn't . . .

Been born prematurely on my mom's birthday with a hole in my heart, I might never have sought to heal an old soul wound.

Witnessed my mom's unexpected and catastrophic illness and the women who accompanied her to the end of her life, I might not have conceived the idea of Hannah.

Said yes to a soul I heard calling, I would have missed out on one of the most loving relationships I've ever known.

Experienced the deaths of my parents and grandparents at a relatively young age, I wouldn't have been as prepared to lose a child.

Taken college classes in death and dying or a hospice volunteer course, I might not have known what to expect at the end of my daughter's life.

Gone through the hell of Hannah's treatments, I might not have become the resilient mother bear that I am now when it comes to defending the needs and feelings of my friends or my adult sons.

Suffered through Hannah's death, I might never have opened my heart to other women who knew a similar loss.

Reached out to other women friends, new and old, I wouldn't have known the depth of bonds between soul sisters.

Survived my daughter's death, I would not have grown tougher and more determined to keep the people in my life who truly meant something to me and let go of the ones who didn't.

Reached out to astrologer and teacher Steve Forrest, I wouldn't have known the depth of purpose Hannah's life had, nor would I have become as good an astrologer.

Discovered George, Heather, or Suzanne and their messages from beyond the veil, or been open to Isabel's "resurrection" story, I wouldn't have found proof of an afterlife, let alone hear from my daughter after her death.

Felt the depth and pain of Hannah's leaving, I wouldn't be as sensitive to others' grief.

Loved Hannah as much as I did, I wouldn't have been as good a mother, wife, grandmother, or friend.

Been Hannah's mother, my heart and soul wouldn't have grown as much.

✤ ✤ ✤

I have wondered if I was born partially broken in order to heal my heart in some way. Maybe when my life here is over, I'll have the answer to some of these questions: *Did something happen to me in a previous life to hurt my heart? Did I come into this life with a heart so overburdened and depleted with cares and responsibilities from a past life? Did my soul long to reconnect with another whom I had known in a previous life? Was Hannah one of those souls? Was the hole in my heart at birth evidence of a wounded soul and a place from which I would heal?*

I know that Hannah was born to heal my heart. Hannah's soul brought me immeasurable joy and unspeakable sorrow. I have known the worst loss, followed by the most extraordinary gifts. From the tragedy of my mom's passing, which inspired Hannah's existence, to the miraculous experiences that followed my daughter's death, I have been blessed.

My heart will always have a Hannah-shaped hole in it. And as her soul lives on, my heart will continue to beat until we meet again in the hereafter.

Bill and Hannah at Cannon Beach,
Oregon, 2006

Hannah and I at her brother's baseball
game

Bill and I today

Acknowledgments

To Bill Hunt, my husband, fellow crisis partner, and supportive companion, for walking with me through this journey and more, for believing in me as a writer to share our daughter's story, and for contributing your beautiful sunflower oil painting to the cover of this book.

To our sons, Ryan and Andrew, for the loving kindness you showed toward Hannah and each other. I'm especially grateful to you for sacrificing part of your adolescence and privacy as you witnessed Hannah's illness and death firsthand. I hope the memory of her warrior spirit helps you to fight for the life you were meant to live.

To our oldest son, Adam, and his wife, Alexis, who were with Hannah to the end. Thank you for the gift of our grandchildren, whom I cherish.

To my mom, for inspiring me to have Hannah. I only wish you could have held her in person.

To my dad, whose life was cut far too short when we were just getting to know each other. Thank you for being our guardian angel.

To my sister, Linda, for gracing me with your wisdom, your loving presence, and your undying loyalty.

To my brother, Claude, for being there for me from the beginning, for literally running beside me, and for challenging me to take care of myself.

To Alli Bannerman Beattie for being the best big sister a kid could ever hope for.

To my Thursday afternoon happy hour group—Jeanette Smith, Jen Parker, Barb Wyatt, Nancy Silverman, and Patti Beer—who have been there since we held our first babies. Thank you for your undying love and support.

To the Shitty First Draft Writing Group: Robin Gaphni, Karen Gerstenberger, Stefanie Kimzey, and Teri Waag. I wouldn't have survived without your comforting company and the inspiration you gave me to write Hannah's story. Before we agree to the next life, Stefanie, we'll have to talk about it!

To the other bereaved moms who have held me up since Hannah passed:

To Molly Greist for your sage advice and for holding my hand while hiking miles with me in search of Hannah's Rock.

To Mary Jane Boxer for your wicked sense of humor, introducing me to George Anderson, and your desire to see that kids diagnosed with brain tumors in the future have a fighting chance.

To Margo Fowkes for being a fellow cancer warrior mother, a fierce advocate, an excellent writer, and the creator of the Salt Water website that supports many others through their grief.

To Claire Barnett, earth mother and wise healer, for giving me an artistic channel to creatively transform my grief into beautiful mosaic garden stones.

To Isabel for your invaluable messages from Hannah, for inviting me to look beyond the veil, and for our shared love of astrology.

To Kathi McMahon, for always offering a comforting ear, for inspiring me to be my physical best, and for having the courage to share your dreams with me.

To the Cheney and Brusseau families for welcoming me into your hearts and into your family.

To my other soul sisters and brothers—you know who you are—for showing up and being present through *all* of it.

To Steve Forrest, wise astrological counselor and teacher, for fostering my life's work, for supporting me as Hannah left her earthly body, and for helping me to understand why she came here in the first place.

To Andrea Conlon, my first astrology teacher and counselor, for recognizing that I had a gift for this ancient art, for introducing me to a wealth of resources, and for encouraging my writing.

To Jennifer Louden and the women at the Vermont writer's retreats, for believing in me as a writer, and for giving me a safe space in which to explore my stories.

To Suzanne Giesemann, for having the courage to follow her heart's mission, for sharing with others that our souls do not end, and for giving me further evidence from Hannah that she is still right here with me.

To the compassionate, brilliant human Dr. Jim Olson, for your efforts to try to save Hannah, for your support of Bill and me when it was clear that that was not possible, and for giving us a cause to fight for via Hannah's Hopeful Hearts.

To Dr. Russ Geyer, nurse practitioner Cory Hoeppner, and nurse Faith Cozier at Seattle Children's Hospital, who headed up Hannah's oncology team, for your kindness and honesty toward Hannah and us, for your valiant efforts to pursue every medical option, and for patiently listening to me when I was desperately trying to find another treatment to save her life.

To Bill Harper, Ann Strickland, and the people of Grace Church for your prayers, your music, and your unconditional support of Hannah and all children affected by pediatric cancer.

To Sue Steindorf, Linda Raquer, Maureen Wilson, and the other therapists and teachers who helped Hannah regain her strength, calm, and dignity: your work and service were a gift of love.

To Erin Austin, artist and composer of "Safe," for sharing your music and for opening my eyes to a way to give back to the childhood cancer world.

To astrologer Linda "Moonrabbit" Zlotnick, for your reading of Hannah's death chart, for introducing me to editor Beth Wright, and for encouraging me to write this story.

To Teri Waag and Nancy Silverman, dear friends and literary women, who were my beta readers as I began to find my voice and revise my manuscript.

And my gratitude to those esteemed colleagues who read my book and offered beautiful endorsements.

To professional photographer Deanna Dusabek for working with me to achieve a natural and beautiful author photo.

To Nancy Silk, copyeditor extraordinaire, for polishing and perfecting this manuscript in its early drafts and for your belief in the story I wanted to tell.

To Beth Wright, project manager and developmental editor, for challenging me to hone my writing skills, for setting the bar high for me to tell an emotional story, and for providing a team of experts who helped me see this book through to its final publication.

To Hannah's friends—especially Lindsay, Shaine, Courtney, Jade, Riley, Sophia, Kajsa, Fiona, and Shania—who were the best best friends a girl could have.

And to Hannah, my beloved daughter, to infinity and beyond, with all my heart.

Sources

Austin, Erin. "Safe." *Home.* Performed by OK Sweetheart. Album produced by Rob Gungor. Riptide Music, 2011.

Cacciatore, Joanne. *Bearing the Unbearable: Love, Loss, and the Heartbreaking Path of Grief.* Somerville, MA: Wisdom Publications, 2017.

Callanan, Maggie, and Patricia Kelley. *Final Gifts: Understanding the Special Awareness, Needs, and Communications of the Dying.* New York: Poseidon Press, 1992.

Frye, Mary Elizabeth. "Do Not Stand at My Grave and Weep." 1932. www.familyfriendpoems.com/poem/do-not-stand-by-my-grave-and-weep-by-mary-elizabeth-frye.

Kübler-Ross, Elisabeth. *On Life After Death.* Berkeley: Celestial Arts, 2008.

Wolterstorff, Nicholas. *Lament for a Son.* Grand Rapids, MI: Eerdmans, 1987.

CPSIA information can be obtained
at www.ICGtesting.com
Printed in the USA
FSHW021012041121
85983FS